Beyond the Twin Deficits

Beyond the Twin Deficits

A Trade Strategy for the 1990s

Robert A. Blecker

M. E. Sharpe, Inc.
Armonk, New York
London, England

Available in the United Kingdom and Europe from M.E. Sharpe,
Publishers, 3 Henrietta Street, London WC2E 8LU.

Library of Congress Cataloging-in-Publication Data

Beyond the twin deficits: A trade strategy for the 1990s / Robert A. Blecker
p.   cm.
Includes bibliographical references and index.
ISBN 1-56324-090-4 — ISBN 1-56324-091-2 (pbk.)
1. Balance of trade—United States.
2. Budget deficits—United States.
3. United States—Commercial policy.
4. Industry and state—United States.
5. Monetary policy—United States.
6. Cost and standard of living—United States.
I. Title
HF3031.B54 1992
382'. 17'0973—dc20
92-9033
CIP

Printed in the United States of America

The paper used in this publication meets the minimum
requirements of American National Standard for
Information Sciences—Permanence of Paper for Printed
Library Materials, ANSIZ39.48-1984

♾

MV 10 9 8 7 6 5 4 3 2 1

Dedication

To my parents,
Luba A. Krasnov-Rein
and Sol Blecker.

TABLE OF CONTENTS

Acknowledgments _____

The author would like to thank Jeff Faux, David Frankel, Lawrence Mishel, Kevin Quinn, Edith Rasell, and William Spriggs of EPI as well as Ron Blackwell, Paul Davidson, Robert Eisner, James Galbraith, Alan Isaac, Robert Lawrence, William Lovett, Thomas Michl, Robert Pollin, Lee Price, Dominick Salvatore, and Tony Thirlwall for comments on earlier drafts. He would also like to thank Lory Camba for superb research assistance. The author alone is responsible for the views expressed here as well as any remaining errors.

Many thanks to EPI Publications Director Danielle M. Currier for her assistance in the copy-editing and production of the final manuscript and to Mid Atlantic/Type 2000 for the typesetting and design.

The Economic Policy Institute is grateful for the support of the Kearny Foundation in making this publication possible.

Executive
Summary

This report challenges the widely held view that the U.S. trade deficit is entirely a result of domestic macro-economic factors, especially the federal government budget deficit. The assumption that trade imbalances are strictly macroeconomic phenomena has led U.S. policymakers to reject industrial and trade strategies aimed at making the nation more competitive in world markets, leaving the country with only one response—reductions in the real incomes of most Americans.

The analysis in this report shows that the assumptions on which current policy rests are flawed both logically and factually. The competitiveness of U.S. industries, both in terms of cost and quality, does have an impact on the U.S. trade balance, and declining competitiveness has contributed significantly to the persistently high trade deficits of the past decade. Contrary to the conventional view of the relationship between the "twin deficits" (budget and trade)—or between the national saving rate and the trade balance—the causality can run *both* ways. That is, poor trade performance or low foreign demand can cause *both* a widening trade deficit *and* a low national saving rate (including a high fiscal deficit), as well as the reverse. This implies the need for industrial and trade policies to improve the performance of U.S.-based industries as well as macroeconomic policy corrections which go beyond mere budget deficit reduction. Only by combining structural and macro policies can the United States find a high-income, high-growth path to trade balance adjustment.

Increased budget deficits did contribute to the growing trade deficits of the early 1980s. But the *highest* estimates of this effect are that *less than half* of the rise in the trade

Only by combining structural and macro policies can the United States find a high-income . . . path to trade balance adjustment.

1

deficit at that time can be explained by the rise in the budget deficit. And macroeconomic factors alone cannot explain the *persistence* of the trade deficit into the early 1990s.

This book documents clear and compelling evidence for a declining trend in the international competitiveness of U.S. industry. The evidence includes the following main points:

- As of 1990, the real value of the U.S. dollar had returned to about its 1980 level, making U.S. products no less competitive in *price* terms than they were ten years earlier. And over the 1980–1990 decade as a whole, foreign incomes grew at least as rapidly as U.S. national income, implying that the U.S. trade deficit could no longer be blamed on more rapid growth in this country. Thus, the effects of expansionary U.S. fiscal policy on the value of the dollar and on the level of U.S. aggregate demand (relative to other countries) had been reversed or neutralized. Nevertheless, the trade deficit was roughly $100 billion *higher* in 1990 than in 1980 (in current dollars), representing a decline of about 2 percent of the gross national product (GNP).

- During the 1970s, a continuous fall in the real value of the dollar (at an annual rate of 2.7 percent) kept the U.S. current account (the broadest measure of the trade balance) roughly balanced, and prevented the real merchandise trade deficit from growing. When the dollar ceased to fall at this rate in the 1980s—and, indeed, rose in 1980–85 before falling again in 1985–1990—the merchandise trade and current account balances both turned sharply negative. *Thus the U.S. has been unable to keep its trade balance from deteriorating without continuously depreciating the dollar in real terms.*

- When U.S. national income rises by 10 percent, U.S. demand for imports rises by about 25 percent. But when foreign incomes rise by 10 percent, foreign demand for U.S. exports rises by only about 15 percent. These unequal "income elasticities" of demand for U.S. imports and exports imply that, in the absence of continuous real dollar depreciation, *the U.S. cannot grow as fast as its trading partners without risking a perpetually widening trade deficit.*

- U.S. nonoil imports rose by about 3 percent per year faster in 1980–89 than can be explained by macroeco-

The U.S. has been unable to keep its trade balance from deteriorating without continuously depreciating the dollar.

nomic variables such as exchange rates, relative prices, and national income (or domestic expenditures). Cumulated over the period 1980–89, this structural trend increase in import demand adds up to about $98 billion (in constant 1982 dollars)—which accounts for nearly all of the remaining trade deficit in 1990. This finding also implies that *the greatest loss of competitiveness occurred on the import side.*

- All of these negative trends in U.S. trade have occurred despite that fact that U.S. wages have been falling relative to those of most other industrial countries (Canada, Japan, and Western Europe), and real wages for American workers have not increased at all (and, on an hourly basis, have even fallen) since the late 1970s.

Economists often argue that any declining trend in U.S. competitiveness will be automatically offset by dollar depreciation in the long run, and therefore there is no need for the government to adopt industrial or trade policies to counteract the decline. The record of exchange rate fluctuations in the past decade gives us little confidence that such an automatic adjustment process will take place. But even if the dollar did adjust to a lower real value, this adjustment would be accompanied by a lower standard of living for all Americans because they would have to pay more for imported goods (as well as goods which compete with imports or which use imported inputs).

Policies designed to improve micro-level industrial performance and open foreign markets would allow the U.S. to achieve greater trade deficit reduction at a lower cost in macroeconomic adjustment (budget cuts, dollar depreciation, etc.). In other words, improved competitiveness lessens the amount of domestic sacrifice required (through fiscal belt-tightening and higher import costs) to balance trade.

In order to analyze U.S. competitive difficulties in greater depth, this report identifies three main groups of countries which disproportionately accounted for the rise in the U.S. trade deficit in the 1980s: the industrialized surplus countries (mainly Germany and Japan), the East Asian newly industrializing countries (the NICs, led by South Korea and Taiwan), and the Latin American debtors (principally Mexico and Brazil). *The underlying structural problems are found to be different in each case,*

Even if the dollar did adjust to a lower real value, this adjustment would be accompanied by a lower standard of living for all Americans.

3

thus calling for a differentiated set of policy responses by the U.S.

In regard to the *industrialized surplus countries,* the underlying problem is the relatively sluggish growth of U.S. productivity, combined with a loss of technological leadership in critical industries. And in the case of Japan, these problems are exacerbated by the closed markets and industrial targeting which have made Japan's trade surplus relatively unresponsive to exchange rate adjustments. For the advanced industrialized nations, this report recommends that the U.S. adopt industrial policies that can help revive productivity growth and technological innovation in U.S. industry. In addition, the U.S. should impose a surcharge on Japanese imports unless Japan effectively opens its market more to U.S. manufactured exports.

In regard to the *East Asian NICs,* the problem lies mainly in their competitive advantage in unit labor costs in manufacturing. This advantage derives from a combination of technology transfers which have raised their labor productivity, domestic policies that have repressed their real wages, and managed exchange rates that have kept their currencies undervalued relative to the dollar. The primary objective of U.S. policy toward those NICs which have persistent balance-of-payments surpluses and large accumulations of international reserves should be to induce them to raise their average manufacturing unit labor costs in dollar terms by some combination of currency revaluation and wage increases. In order to induce such a policy shift, the U.S. should threaten to impose an import surcharge which would equalize average unit labor costs in manufacturing—thus making wage differentials in dollar terms reflect average productivity differentials. The NICs should prefer to revalue their currencies rather than accept the surcharge, since the former will improve their terms of trade (purchasing power over imports) while the latter will not.

For the *Latin American debtors,* the biggest problem since 1982 has been their inability to obtain net inflows of foreign capital to finance both domestic investment and imports. In fact, Latin America became a net exporter of capital as it was forced to transfer resources to the creditor nations in order to service the existing debts (or at least to buy needed imports) with few new capital inflows. Greater debt relief is needed to overcome this

> *In the case of Japan, these problems are exacerbated by . . . closed markets and industrial targeting.*

4

problem in order to allow Latin American countries once again to become net importers of capital and goods from the U.S. and other industrial countries. A free trade agreement with Mexico or other Latin American countries would not be helpful for solving the U.S. trade imbalance, however, as it would only encourage more foreign investment in low-wage production for export to the U.S. market.

Finally, although domestic macroeconomic policies alone cannot solve the trade deficit at an acceptable social cost, sensible macro policies are still important ingredients in an overall policy package for trade. The dollar should be brought down to and held at a level which would make U.S. goods competitive with the products of Europe and Japan, either through international coordination (such as with target zones) or, if the Europeans (especially the Germans) and Japanese will not go along, through a unilateral low interest rate policy. However, continuous dollar depreciation could have deleterious effects and should be avoided. Foreign countries should be encouraged to continue the relatively rapid growth they had in the late 1980s in order to relieve the pressure for the U.S. to be the sole "engine of growth" in the world economy (as it was in the early 1980s). Any reductions in the U.S. budget deficit should be gradual, and phased in after the recovery from the current recession is well under way.

Finally, any fiscal policy adjustments need to be tailored to reverse two adverse trends of recent decades: the decline in public sector investment spending and the decreasing progressivity of the tax code. The argument that the budget and trade deficits are twins overemphasizes the size of the budget deficit and overlooks the composition of federal spending, thus rationalizing fiscal cutbacks which starve the very national investments in education, training, and infrastructure that are needed in order to improve the country's competitiveness. And the twin deficits argument also ignores the fact that the fiscal policies which contributed to the trade deficit did so largely by reducing the tax burden on capital income and the richest families in the country.

Sensible macro policies are still important ingredients in an overall policy package for trade.

Introduction

In 1990, the U.S. merchandise trade deficit topped $100 billion for the seventh consecutive year. To be sure, the 1990 deficit of $108.7 billion was about one-third lower than the 1987 record deficit of $159.5 billion,[1] and was exacerbated by the temporary rise in oil prices following the Iraqi invasion of Kuwait. But even the modest improvement in the nonoil part of the trade balance in recent years came at a steep price: a substantial fall in the value of the U.S. dollar from its 1985 peak, falling average hourly wages (after correcting for inflation), and a slowdown in U.S. economic growth culminating in the recession which began in late 1990.

Fundamentally, what is at stake is the ability of the United States to provide sustainable increases in the standard of living of its people in the future.

The fact that a still historically large trade deficit persists even after such "adjustments" indicates the presence of structural problems underlying poor U.S. trade performance. These problems include foreign trade policies and institutional barriers which restrict demand for U.S. exports. But the largest part of the problem lies in a declining trend in the competitiveness of U.S. products relative to foreign substitutes. This trend shows up especially in the fact that U.S. imports have grown more rapidly in recent years than we would expect based on the growth of U.S. incomes and the relative prices of imports. Such an unfavorable trend does not mean that the United States cannot balance its trade, but it does imply that we cannot do so without more painful adjustments: some combination of further declines in the purchasing power of the dollar, greater erosion of real wages, and slower income growth in the future.

Fundamentally, what is at stake is the ability of the United States to provide sustainable increases in the standard of living of its people in the future. In fact, the material well-being of most American families has improved little if at all in the past decade, although the wealthiest households have done extremely well (see Blecker, 1990a; Mishel and Frankel, 1991). But even this unequal and disappointing performance has come at the expense of chronic trade deficits, implying that our total spending exceeds our national income. Sustainable increases in living standards—especially for the middle- and lower-income families who have been left behind in the past decade—will not be possible unless the nation's domestic productivity slowdown and international competitive decline are reversed.

The emergence of chronic trade deficits in the past decade has been linked to the growing inequality in American society, both as cause and effect. On the one hand, rising import penetration in manufacturing has contributed to the decline in high-wage jobs and thus to the phenomenon of the "disappearing middle" in the distribution of income (see Mishel and Teixeira, 1991).[2] On the other hand, the fiscal policy changes that are generally regarded as having contributed to the trade deficit, especially the Reagan tax cuts of the early 1980s, were highly regressive in their effects on income distribution. Thus the much-touted rise in the "structural budget deficit" and the concomitant fall in the national saving rate (public plus private) were products of the *same* fiscal policy changes that redistributed after-tax income upward.

This study will examine the evidence for the existence of a structural declining trend in U.S. competitiveness, as well as analyze the contribution of this and other factors to U.S. trade problems in general and the trade deficit in particular. In addition, this study will suggest some trade and other types of policies which could be used to lessen the burden of trade balance adjustment on U.S. workers and consumers, while helping to revive economic growth without a return to rising trade deficits. The point is to reduce the cost of balancing trade by addressing the underlying structural deficiencies and obstacles rather than to design policies that will balance trade at any cost. In particular, the intention is to find avenues for solving trade problems which can alleviate, rather than worsen, the slow growth of family incomes and the rising inequality of income distribution in this country.

This focus is clearly different from the commonly held

8

view that the U.S. trade deficit is merely a "twin" of the federal government budget deficit, and that the only thing we can or should do to reduce the former is to "get our own house in order" by reducing the latter. For example, the 1990 *Economic Report of the President* claims that the "best means" for reducing the U.S. trade deficit is by "reducing the federal budget deficit and taking steps to raise private saving"[3] (p. 98). Such an extreme view of the twin deficits, while often accepted by editorialists and pundits, is not necessarily supported by serious economic research. But there is a consensus among many economists that macroeconomic policies, more broadly defined, are largely to blame for the U.S. trade deficit, and that among these, the federal budget deficit is the primary (if not the exclusive) culprit.[4]

[The] persistence of the trade deficit indicates an underlying decline in competitiveness.

It is undeniable that shifts in macro policies have had a significant impact on the trade balance in the past decade. But this does not mean that there was no underlying declining trend in the trade balance due to deteriorating competitiveness. In the early 1980s, one could plausibly claim that macroeconomic factors, broadly defined, accounted for most of the increase in the U.S. trade deficit. But since most of these factors were largely reversed or neutralized in the late 1980s, the effects of these policies alone cannot account for the persistence of large trade deficits into the early 1990s.

Macro policies affect the trade balance through their effects on U.S. income growth (relative to foreign income growth) and the exchange value of the dollar (which affects relative prices of U.S. and foreign goods). In 1982–84, U.S. national income grew faster than foreign countries' incomes, while the value of the dollar soared from 1980–85. Over the 1980s as a whole, however, U.S. income growth was no more rapid than that of most other countries, as more expansionary macro policies in other countries offset the expansionary U.S. fiscal deficit. And by 1990 the dollar had returned to about its 1980 value. Yet the trade deficit in 1990 stood well above its 1980 level both in real (inflation-adjusted) terms and as a percentage of gross national product (GNP). Even some who emphasize conventional macroeconomic explanations for the trade deficit acknowledge that this persistence of the trade deficit indicates an underlying decline in competitiveness (e.g., Lawrence, 1990).

While the twin deficit view implies an automatic and

direct connection between the budget deficit and the trade deficit, the actual relationship between the two deficits is much more complex than this view allows. For one thing, the extent to which U.S. government deficit spending spills over into a foreign trade deficit depends on a number of conditions which are not themselves products of fiscal policies. Chief among these conditions is the relative attractiveness of domestic and foreign products, both in terms of cost and quality, which determines whether the extra incomes generated by the government deficit are spent at home or abroad.

Moreover, the actual size of the budget deficit—or even of the "structural" (cyclically-adjusted) deficit—is not entirely a reflection of fiscal policies (tax rates and spending levels), but also of the productivity and competitiveness of the economy insofar as these affect the levels of domestic production and national income subject to taxation. Thus, there may be some degree of *reverse causality* in that declining competitiveness makes it harder for the government to balance its budget, as well as for the nation to balance its trade. Further, the effects of fiscal policies on trade depend on more than just the size of the gap between revenue and outlays. For example, the percentage of government expenditures which is allocated to public investment can have a positive impact on private productivity, and thus on competitiveness (see Aschauer, 1990). For both these reasons, it is especially perverse to try to reduce the "twin deficits" by cutting public investment spending.[5]

In addition, American fiscal policies are only one part of the macro policy picture. By depressing foreign demand for U.S. exports, contractionary macro policies in the industrialized surplus countries (Japan, West Germany) and the Latin American debtors also contributed significantly to the increased U.S. trade deficit in the 1980s. And the generally tight monetary policy of the U.S. Federal Reserve in the 1980s had an independent effect in keeping real interest rates high, thus attracting funds into U.S. financial markets. This raised the value of the dollar in 1980–85, and limited its fall in 1987–89. By overvaluing the dollar, the monetary policies of the 1980s priced U.S. goods out of markets both at home and abroad—something that the budget deficit by itself would not have done. In addition, high interest rates appear to have contributed to both the upper-class per-

> By overvaluing the dollar, the monetary policies of the 1980s priced U.S. goods out of markets both at home and abroad.

10

sonal consumption binge (which fuels the trade deficit) and the declining reinvestment of corporate profits in industrial production (which undercuts competitiveness).[6]

The purpose of this study is thus not to deny the effects that macro policies have had on trade, but rather to develop a broader framework for analyzing the nation's trade problems. In broadening the scope of analysis, we are led to investigate bilateral relationships between the United States and its main trading partners. Since competitiveness is inherently a relative concept, the decline in U.S. competitiveness must be analyzed in relation to those countries that have gained competitiveness relative to the United States. This makes it necessary to consider bilateral trade relations between the United States and two major groups of countries: the technologically-advanced industrial surplus countries (principally Japan and West Germany), and the East Asian newly industrializing countries (NICs) with large trade surpluses (especially South Korea and Taiwan).

The greatest structural trade problems by far are those with Japan.

Among the industrialized countries, the greatest structural trade problems by far are those with Japan. Japan's closed markets and successful targeting of exports are well-documented (see Salvatore, 1990). Unlike all other industrialized nations, Japan has not increased its imports of manufactured goods in proportion to its national income in recent decades (Dornbusch, 1990). And the U.S. trade deficit with Japan has remained stubbornly high in spite of a major depreciation of the dollar against the yen since 1985.

In contrast, the United States now has a small trade surplus with Western Europe, as deficits with Germany and Italy were offset by surpluses with most other European countries in 1990. Nevertheless, this balanced trade with Europe has been bought only through the depreciation of the dollar against the European currencies and a fall in U.S. wages relative to European wages. Thus, while the trade balance with Europe has been more susceptible to conventional "adjustments" than the deficit with Japan, the nature of these adjustments still reveals a decline in U.S. competitiveness vis-à-vis Europe as well as Japan. This decline is also independently verified by indicators which show Europe and Japan catching up to (or surpassing) the United States in labor productivity and technological innovation.

11

In regard to developing countries, the greatest U.S. trade problems are with the supercompetitive[7] NICs of East Asia. By holding down wage increases relative to productivity growth and keeping their currencies undervalued, countries such as South Korea and Taiwan have made their exports artificially cheap and have engaged in a "beggar-thy-neighbor" form of export-led growth which exports unemployment to deficit countries like the U.S. In addition, the Latin American economies—which traditionally served as major markets for U.S. exports—have been crippled in the last decade by the effects of the debt crisis. These nations have had to drastically curtail their imports from the United States—especially imports of capital goods which are critical to U.S. technological progress—while engaging in a crash effort to promote low-wage manufactured exports on the East Asian model.

> **For our trade with the industrialized nations . . . we mainly need industrial policies to promote the development of our high-tech sectors and the diffusion of advanced technologies.**

Reducing the trade deficit at an acceptable cost requires specific measures addressed to our structural problems with each of these major trading partners. Different types of policies, both external and internal, are indicated in each case. For our trade with the industrialized nations, which is largely driven by absolute technological advantages, we mainly need industrial policies to promote the development of our high-tech sectors and the diffusion of advanced technologies into "mature" industries. In addition, special trade measures may be needed to open up the Japanese market and to subject Japan to common "rules of the game" in harmony with the United States and the European Community (EC). A moderately low dollar can help to promote exports to these countries, or at least serve as a lever to pry open closed markets and induce more expansionary foreign macro policies. But too much dollar depreciation would not be helpful, especially because it would remove the incentives for U.S. producers to "upscale" in quality and productivity (Porter, 1990).

For our trade with the supercompetitive NICs, we must support the efforts of their workers to obtain a greater share of their productivity gains in the form of higher wages, while pressuring their governments to allow their currencies to appreciate to levels more consistent with balanced trade. For those countries like Korea and Taiwan which have amassed enormous dollar reserves and net foreign assets while keeping their currencies undervalued, we should be willing to impose an import surcharge

12

designed to equalize their average unit labor costs in manufacturing (converted to dollars) with ours. Hopefully, the mere threat of such a surcharge would induce them to revalue their currencies and/or allow wage increases sufficient to make actual imposition of the surcharge unnecessary.

In regard to Latin America, the primary focus should be on greater debt relief and efforts to revive their internal growth and development—which would help workers and firms on both sides of the Rio Grande. Trade liberalization alone, as envisioned in the proposed U.S.-Mexico Free Trade Agreement, would only encourage mutually destructive competition in the form of low wages, unhealthful working conditions, and environmental degradation.

Although the primary concern of this report is with trade in manufactures, it is important to take note of the fact that oil imports represent a chronic drain on the U.S. balance of payments. The United States cannot achieve overall balanced trade unless it runs a nonoil surplus large enough to offset the oil deficit, which totaled $54.6 billion in 1990 (U.S. Department of Commerce, Census Bureau, Foreign Trade Division, Report FT990, December 1990). The Persian Gulf crisis provided an opportune reminder of U.S. economic vulnerability to oil price "shocks." A coherent U.S. trade policy must therefore also include a coherent energy policy aimed at reducing dependence on imported oil. This report suggests that such a policy should operate mainly by encouraging energy conservation rather than by stimulating more energy production at home.

The rest of this report is organized as follows. Chapter 1 discusses how changes in international competitiveness affect the foreign trade balance and the domestic standard of living. This chapter also analyzes the risks of relying on exchange rate adjustments to offset competitive advantages or disadvantages, as well as the limits to income growth implied by a lack of competitiveness. Chapter 2 critically evaluates the conventional view that the trade deficit is purely a result of macroeconomic policies. The chapter concludes that less than half of the rise in the U.S. trade deficit in the early 1980s can be attributed to the increased U.S. budget deficit at that time, and that virtually none of the remaining trade deficit today can be attributed to differences in U.S. versus foreign mac-

We should be willing to impose an import surcharge designed to equalize [the NICs'] average unit labor costs in manufacturing (converted to dollars) with ours.

roeconomic policies. Chapter 2 also analyzes the contribution of monetary policy to the gyrations in the value of the dollar and the resulting effects on U.S. trade.

Chapter 3 then presents three kinds of evidence for a declining trend of U.S. competitiveness. First, there is a declining trend in the value of the dollar which would be consistent with balanced trade. Second, domestic demand for U.S. imports is stronger than foreign demand for U.S. exports, as measured by "income elasticities." And third, it is estimated that nonoil merchandise imports rose from 1980 to 1989 by $98 billion more (in constant 1982 dollars) than can be explained by conventional macroeconomic variables. The econometric evidence for the latter two propositions is presented in a technical Appendix. Chapter 4 shows how the decline in U.S. trade performance is reflected in a reduced global market share for manufactured exports, and that the rise in the trade deficit is largely accounted for by a relatively small group of countries. Chapter 4 also presents a conceptual framework for analyzing the causes of changing U.S. trade relations with different types of countries, both developed and less developed.

Chapters 5 and 6 give more detailed analyses of U.S. bilateral trade relations with major trading partners. Specifically, Chapter 5 considers the causes and consequences of our declining competitiveness relative to Japan and the EC, emphasizing diminishing American technological leadership as well as the special "structural impediments" which characterize the Japanese market. Chapter 6 analyzes U.S. trade problems with developing nations, both the East Asian NICs and the Latin American debtors. Finally, Chapter 7 presents policy conclusions, both for internal reforms in the United States and for forging more balanced relationships with some of our trading partners.

Nonoil merchandise imports rose from 1980 to 1989 by $98 billion more than can be explained by conventional macroeconomic variables.

Endnotes

1   Data are from the U.S. Department of Commerce, Bureau of Economic Analysis (BEA), as published in *Economic Indicators*, February 1991; the figure for 1990 is preliminary.

2   For an analysis of how changes in international competitiveness have affected relative wages at the industry level, see Galbraith and Calmon (forthcoming).

3   "Steps to raise private saving" is, in this context, just a euphemism for cutting capital gains taxes. But most objective analyses show that cutting capital gains taxes would raise the federal budget deficit over a five-year period (Quinn, 1990).

4   For a survey of the literature on the U.S. trade deficit which emphasizes the consensus view, see Hooper and Mann (1989b). Not all economists share in this consensus, however. For alternative viewpoints, see, for example, Hufbauer (1985), Price (1986), Lovett (1988), Dewald and Ulan (1990), and Eisner and Pieper (1990, 1992).

5   For these reasons, it is clearly counterproductive for the Bush administration to ask Japan (which already has a much higher percentage of its national product devoted to public investment than the U.S.) to *increase* its public investment spending as a way of removing "structural impediments" to U.S.-Japan trade. Such an increase would only enhance Japan's structural advantages, especially when coupled with public investment cutbacks in the U.S. under the name of "deficit reduction."

6   See Cantor (1989), Blecker (1990a, 1991a), and Blair and Litan (1990).

7   I am indebted to James Galbraith for suggesting this phrase.

Chapter 1

Competitiveness, Trade, and Incomes

Many economists argue that the trade deficit is merely the result of macroeconomic factors, such as the U.S. budget deficit, and has little or no relationship to the competitiveness of U.S. products. In this view, competitiveness only affects the composition of trade (e.g., whether steel is an import or an export), but not the overall level of trade or the trade balance. For example, two economists from The Brookings Institution wrote:

> There is no mystery about the causes of the swelling U.S. external deficit. They are chiefly macroeconomic. Other causes commonly said to be important, such as "unfair trading practices" abroad or structural changes in the U.S. and foreign economies, simply do not explain most of what has happened. (Bryant and Holtham, 1987, p. 28)

Two other leading international economists have argued that "Most trade and productivity policies will have insignificant long-run effects on the trade deficit because they have minimal effects on macroeconomic conditions" (McCulloch and Richardson, 1986, p. 51).

However, some economists have qualified their arguments on this point in ways which effectively admit that competitiveness *can* matter to the trade balance (or to the broader current account in the balance of payments). Thus, Eichengreen (1988) wrote that:

> The current account is a macroeconomic variable determined by relationships among other macroeconomic variables, notably by any imbalance between savings and

Many economists argue that the trade deficit is merely the result of macroeconomic factors, such as the U.S. budget deficit.

17

investment. Thus, the current account deficit results ultimately from those macroeconomic policies influencing aggregate savings and investment behavior. Developments affecting particular industries determine only the composition of the current account, not its level. *Trends in the basic industries influence the current account only insofar as their prospects affect the economywide investment climate or their performance affects economywide levels of employment and profitability sufficiently to alter the aggregate level of savings.* (p. 333, italics added)

It will be argued here that this is exactly how competitiveness affects the trade balance as well as the growth of national income and the domestic standard of living.

The argument in this chapter proceeds through three stages: (1) how changes in competitiveness affect the trade balance and other macro variables, for any given exchange value of the dollar; (2) whether exchange rate adjustments can be expected to offset changes in competitiveness, and what are the implications if they do; and (3) how a change in competitiveness affects the relative rates at which income can grow in different countries, if those countries are to sustain balanced trade in the long run.

The Macro Identity

It is useful to begin with a simple but important economic relationship which has often been invoked by those who argue that the trade deficit is caused only by macroeconomic policies. In order to run a trade deficit, a country has to pay for the excess of its imports over its exports either by selling assets (e.g., gold, foreign currency reserves, real estate, or factories) to the rest of the world, or else by borrowing from other countries (i.e., acquiring foreign debts). By the same token, a nation with a trade surplus must either acquire ownership of foreign assets, or else extend credit (lend) to the rest of the world. This means that a nation's trade balance must be equal to the difference between what it saves and what it invests at home:[1]

(1)   Trade Balance = National Saving − Domestic
                                                    Investment.

"National saving" in turn is the sum of private saving (of households and corporations) plus public sector saving (the government's budget surplus). If the government is run-

> Competitiveness affects the trade balance as well as the growth of national income and the domestic standard of living.

ning a budget deficit, then public saving is negative, and national saving is less than private saving. By separating the government budget from private saving, we can rewrite (1) as:

(2) Trade Balance = Private Saving + Budget Surplus
              − Domestic Investment.

The "twin deficits" view assumes that the government budget deficit (negative surplus) on the right-hand side causes a trade deficit (negative balance) on the left. The closely related "saving shortfall" view asserts that both the budget deficit and a low private saving rate are responsible for the trade deficit. For example, three influential economists have argued that:

> **These identities say nothing about the direction of causality.**

> The current low national saving rate. . . lies at the root of both our unprecedented trade deficits and our inadequate level of domestic investment.. . . . *While the budget deficit was an important contributory factor to the decline in national saving in the 1980s, it was far from the whole story: declining private saving was more important.* (Hatsopoulos, Krugman, and Poterba, 1989, p. 6; italics in original)

The argument that the United States has been suffering from a sharp decline in its private saving rate has been criticized elsewhere by this author and by others (see Blecker, 1990a, 1990b, 1991a; Block, 1990; Eisner, 1991; Goldstein, 1990; Lipsey and Kravis, 1987; and Steindl, 1990). However, what concerns us here is the argument that a low national saving rate (including a large budget deficit) must be the root cause of the trade deficit.

The "twin deficit" and "saving shortfall" arguments forget that equations (1) and (2) are merely identities: statements that are tautologically true. By themselves, these identities say nothing about the *direction of causality*— which of the variables (if any) are independent causes of changes in the other variables. As Harvard economist and former Undersecretary of State Richard N. Cooper has written,

> This relationship is an after the fact identity. It represents an important check on the consistency of any proposed policy, since in order to reduce the current account deficit the policy actions must also affect savings and investment in the required way. But *this accounting identity*

19

says nothing about the dynamics of the impact of policy actions on the economy. (Cooper, 1987, p. 12, italics added)

Cooper's point about logical consistency is well-taken: if one wants to argue that structural changes in a nation's international competitive position can affect its trade balance, one must have a convincing explanation of how such changes affect national saving (relative to domestic investment) so as to satisfy the identity (1) or (2). Suppose, then, that a country's trade performance improves as a result of innovations which give domestic products a greater competitive advantage in either quality or cost, or from the opening up of a new foreign market. The immediate effect will be to increase the country's exports or reduce its imports, and thus to improve the trade balance, for any given exchange rate and level of national income. Let us trace exactly how this will affect national saving and domestic investment.

> **Both parts of national saving—private and public—should benefit from greater international competitiveness.**

Assuming that the country has some excess industrial capacity and less-than-full employment, as is normally the case, higher net export demand increases domestic output and employment. As output and employment rise, national income grows. The increased national income will be divided between higher capital and labor incomes; in general, both will increase to some extent. Now these higher incomes in turn result in higher private saving, both corporate and personal. Since corporate saving accounts form the lion's share of gross private saving in the United States, the increase in corporate profits is especially important for total saving to rise.

In addition, higher private incomes imply higher tax revenue for the government, since most taxes are proportional to either income or spending (and spending tends to rise with income). Since government expenditures are unlikely to rise when private incomes increase (and are likely to fall if higher employment lessens social welfare costs), the government budget surplus should increase (the deficit decreases). Thus both parts of national saving—private and public—should benefit from greater international competitiveness.

It is also likely that business investment will be stimulated to some extent by increased consumer demand and higher capacity utilization in industry, as well as by increased corporate profitability (which provides incentives to invest and relieves potential financing constraints).

20

Since increased domestic investment will absorb some part of the increased national saving, the net improvement in the saving-investment balance will be diminished to the extent that investment also rises. However, in a stable macroeconomic system,[2] the induced increase in domestic investment will normally be less than the induced increase in national saving (private saving plus the government surplus). This implies that the right-hand side of identity (1) should increase to some extent as national income (GNP) adjusts to its new higher level.

At the same time, some part of the increased national income will be spent on imports. This "leakage" to imports reduces but does not eliminate the positive gain in the trade balance from improved competitiveness (or access to foreign markets), since only a fraction of every dollar of increased income will be spent on imports. And, the greater the competitiveness of domestic products, the smaller this fraction should be.[3] Thus, an improvement in competitiveness should be expected to raise the equilibrium trade balance *and* national saving relative to domestic investment—thus increasing *both* sides of identity (1)—although the net increase in the trade balance will be somewhat less than the hypothesized initial increase in net exports.

An improvement in competitiveness should be expected to raise the equilibrium trade balance and national saving relative to domestic investment.

In the case of a deterioration in competitiveness, this mechanism will work in reverse. Domestic output and national income will be reduced, employment will fall, and both corporate profits and workers' wages will be lower. Both private saving and government tax revenue should then be expected to fall, thus reducing national saving (by relatively more than investment contracts). The trade balance will worsen, although this effect will be partially mitigated by reduced demand for imports due to lower national income. The government budget surplus will also tend to fall (the deficit to rise), creating an apparent "twin" relationship between the trade and budget deficits—but without a change in fiscal policy being responsible.

The assumptions of excess capacity and less-than-full employment which we have made are actually less restrictive than they may appear.[4] True cases of sustained full utilization and full employment are rare in capitalist economies outside of wartime. Near the end of the recent economic expansion in 1988–89, capacity utilization in U.S. manufacturing reached about 84 percent, while the U.S. civilian unemployment rate hovered just above 5 percent.[5] These

21

rates were far from true exhaustion of the labor force or industrial capacity. In fact, manufacturing capacity itself grew relatively slowly in the 1980s (at an average annual rate of 2.8 percent in 1980–89, compared with 4.4 percent in 1948–1979), partly as a result of high interest rates and the trade deficit. And the moderately high demand conditions of the late 1980s proved to be unsustainable, as the economy sank into recession by the end of 1990. By March 1991, the unemployment rate was back up to 6.8 percent, and capacity utilization had fallen to 77 percent.

> **Better trade performance can help provide "more jobs" as well as "better jobs."**

Many analyses of trade imbalances implicitly assume full employment. For example, this is evidently assumed by McCulloch and Richardson (1986, p. 51) when they assert that improved competitiveness would mean "higher-productivity jobs" but "not necessarily more jobs." If one assumes full employment, then of course "more jobs" are ruled out. But in spite of the tendency among economists to assume that there is always full employment in the "long run," actual advanced capitalist economies tend to oscillate between periods of relatively high and relatively low employment, rather than to stay at full employment unless disturbed. In this case, better trade performance can help provide "more jobs" as well as "better jobs."

Exchange Rate Adjustment and Living Standards

In theory, the positive effects of improved competitiveness just described could be completely offset by a sufficient appreciation of the nation's currency. This would make the country's exports more expensive abroad, while cheapening imports at home. Indeed, this is exactly what is argued by those who claim that competitiveness does not matter to the trade balance:

> ... the ingredients of industrial competitiveness cannot be regarded as *independent* determinants of trade performance. In particular, induced movements in exchange rates tend to offset the aggregate consequences of any improvement in industrial competitiveness. Unless national saving rises relative to the demand for funds for private investment, any increase in the competitiveness of an industry will be accommodated mainly through a *further appreciation* of the dollar.... (McCulloch, 1986, p. 26, italics in original)

The qualifying phrase "Unless national saving rises..." in the last sentence is crucial; as explained above, this is

22

exactly how an increase in competitiveness (or opening up of foreign markets) can improve the trade balance.

While McCulloch implies that exchange rate movements immediately offset changes in competitiveness, Robert Z. Lawrence (1989) takes the more defensible position that such adjustments only occur in the "long run":

> ... changes in the relative trade performance of American industries will only affect the trade balance in the short run. The trade deficit may rise temporarily, but the loss of foreign markets will put downward pressure on U.S. wages and prices, and, more important, will tend to depress the exchange value of the dollar ... to the point where the trade deficit turns around and moves back to an equilibrium determined by the country's fundamental spending-saving behavior. (Lawrence, 1989, p. 29)

In spite of his efforts to emphasize the long-run adjustment mechanism, however, Lawrence effectively concedes that the trade balance *is* affected by industrial competitiveness in the "short run"—defined as the period in which exchange rates have not sufficiently adjusted. Once the problem is posed in this way, however, it becomes relevant to ask: how long is the "short run"? How long will it take for the exchange rate to settle at its new long-run equilibrium level, following a change in competitiveness?

In order for the exchange rate to adjust to a level which would offset competitive advantages (or disadvantages), it is necessary for exchange rate changes to be driven by the need to restore balanced trade. That is, when a country's trade balance improves, its currency would have to appreciate; when a country's trade balance worsens, its currency would have to depreciate. Before flexible exchange rates were adopted in the early 1970s, this is generally how economists anticipated that a system of flexible rates would work. But the reality has turned out to be quite different. Flexible exchange rates are determined by the conditions for *overall* balance-of-payments equilibrium, not balanced merchandise trade or even a balanced current account (which includes trade in services, net interest payments, and unilateral transfers). This means that capital account transactions—i.e., international investment, borrowing, and lending—play an important role in determining currency fluctuations.

In fact, international capital flows have turned out to be far *more* important than current account transactions

Flexible exchange rates are determined by the conditions for overall balance-of-payments equilibrium, not balanced merchandise trade or even a balanced current account.

(trade in goods and services) for determining exchange rates. The sheer volume of international financial flows dwarfs the value of trade flows. According to Levich (1988, p. 220), foreign exchange transactions in the three largest trading centers (London, New York, and Tokyo) alone totaled $188 billion *per day* as of March 1986, and "worldwide foreign exchange could possibly exceed $250 billion per day or more than $60 trillion per year." In contrast, the total value of U.S. merchandise trade (exports plus imports) in 1986 was $592 billion for the entire year, or less than $2 billion per day.

> *There is no simple or automatic way in which exchange rate adjustments may be expected to exactly offset real competitive advantages or disadvantages.*

It is now generally recognized that the main determinants of fluctuations in currency values, at least in the short run, are located in international financial markets, not in international goods markets. This insight led economists in the 1970s to develop theories in which underlying macroeconomic "fundamentals" (such as money supplies, budget deficits, interest rates, and inflation rates) explain changes in exchange rates. By the end of the 1980s, however, international economists had to admit that even these theories could not explain much of the volatility of exchange rates over the preceding two decades. In particular, a number of economists (e.g., Dornbusch, 1988a and 1989b; Frankel, 1990; Krugman, 1989) have concluded that the rise in the U.S. dollar in the mid-1980s went far beyond anything that could be explained by such fundamentals.

In a survey of recent studies of exchange rate behavior, Meese (1990) concluded that the existing theoretical models of exchange rate behavior cannot explain fluctuations in exchange rates better than the naive assumption that they follow a "random walk." New statistical tests have revealed to economists what market participants knew all along: that a large part of foreign exchange transactions are driven by pure speculation—buying currencies which are expected to rise, and selling currencies which are expected to fall. But if currencies can rise or fall partly as a result of speculative bubbles which are largely unpredictable, then there is no simple or automatic way in which exchange rate adjustments may be expected to exactly offset real competitive advantages or disadvantages over any specific time horizon.

To be sure, these conclusions apply only to efforts to explain short-term (high-frequency) fluctuations in exchange rates. Speculative bubbles are, by their nature, temporary, and purely random processes do not necessarily

24

produce sustained departures from exchange rates that would yield balanced trade in the long run. Nevertheless, the new view of exchange rates should give pause to those who assert an automatic tendency for exchange rates to move quickly in the right direction to offset changes in competitiveness. Given the dominance of financial factors and the inherent unpredictability of speculative frenzies and random processes, we cannot even be sure that exchange rates will necessarily move in the right direction—let alone ascertain how long it would take them to reach an "equilibrium" level consistent with balanced trade.

In this light, it is difficult to give credence to assertions such as the following:

> When *one industry's* performance improves, increases in the international value of the dollar and in production costs squeeze out marginal U.S. exports and squeeze in marginal U.S. imports. With no change in saving-investment aggregates, the net result is an offset that leaves the overall trade balance and employment unchanged. (McCulloch and Richardson, 1986, p. 62, italics added)

Given that exchange rates may be relatively insensitive to even large aggregate trade deficits, it seems farfetched to claim that the dollar will rise exactly enough to offset improved competitiveness in any single industry. A much more likely outcome would be that the firms in that industry would experience increased profits, thus stimulating higher corporate saving as well as raising government tax revenue, and improving the trade balance as well.

The assertion that, in the long run, the value of the dollar must adjust to offset any change in real competitive advantages seems to be based on outmoded *a priori* reasoning rather than any evidence on the actual behavior of exchange rates in recent years. Certainly the experience of the 1980s, which will be discussed in more detail in Chapter 3, suggests that the dollar can stay above a level that would be consistent with balanced trade for at least a decade. But if exchange rates do not do their job, then the "short run" can be quite long in practice. *If the dollar does not adjust to its hypothetical "long run" equilibrium value faster than the underlying competitive conditions themselves change, then actual trade deficits can be continuously affected by those conditions for an indefinite period of time.*

Certainly the experience of the 1980s . . . suggests that the dollar can stay above a level that would be consistent with balanced trade for at least a decade.

25

Moreover, *even if the nation's currency does eventually adjust to its new equilibrium value, this new value will reflect the changed competitive conditions*. This point is crucial, because the value of the nation's currency is an important determinant of its cost of living, and therefore of the purchasing power of domestic incomes. To the extent that people consume imported products, or products which are manufactured with imported inputs, a higher value of the currency means a higher standard of living for domestic residents, and a lower value means the opposite. Therefore, even if one is optimistic about the effectiveness of exchange rate adjustment, one should still be concerned about a nation's underlying competitiveness.

> The value of the nation's currency is an important determinant of its cost of living.

This point has been acknowledged in a number of recent studies by prominent economists. Lawrence implicitly accepted this point when he wrote:

In the process [of adjusting to a decline in competitiveness], however, the deterioration in the terms of trade [due to the depreciation of the currency] ... will exert a downward influence on American living standards. (1989, p. 29)

Similarly, Hatsopoulos, Krugman, and Summers (1988) argued that the United States has a serious competitiveness problem, defined as the inability of the country to balance its trade while "achieving an acceptable rate of improvement in its standard of living" (p. 299). The logic is that, if a country is not competitive, it can balance its trade only by depreciating its currency or, equivalently, by cutting its workers' real wages. Competitiveness thus influences the real income level (purchasing power of consumers) which is consistent with balanced trade.

If a country with a trade deficit improves its competitiveness, then the degree of real currency depreciation (or wage cuts) required to balance trade in the long run is reduced, and hence the sacrifice of domestic living standards necessary to restore external balance is diminished. As Dornbusch, Krugman, and Park wrote in their report, *Meeting World Challenges: U.S. Manufacturing in the 1990s* (1989):

The macroeconomic adjustment that the United States faces over the years ahead [in order to reduce the trade deficit] is linked to the microeconomic issues of competitiveness in particular products and the general performance of U.S. exports and import-competing industries.

26

How well we compete will determine how far the dollar needs to fall, which in turn makes a major difference to the costs in terms of our standard of living of bringing our trade deficit down. (p. 9)

In this view, micro-level policies are *essential* to alleviate the future costs of adjustment to the U.S. external imbalance. The more the U.S. can enhance the competitiveness of its own industries, as well as open up markets for its products abroad, the less the dollar and real wages will have to fall in order to eliminate the trade deficit, and the higher will be the sustainable standard of living associated with balanced trade in the long run.

The fact that it can take a long time for the exchange rate adjustment process to work is especially significant because of its dynamic implications. *By the time the exchange rate eventually adjusts, a country is not starting from the same initial conditions as when the competitive improvement (or deterioration) originally occurred.* In the intervening years, the more competitive nation will have invested in more new capital and R&D, increased its labor productivity faster, and raised its technological advantages further, while the less competitive nation will have fallen behind in all these respects.[6] The eventual appreciation or depreciation of the currency will not necessarily be sufficient to reverse these dynamic gains or losses, and therefore will not return a country's economy to the position it was in before the change in competitiveness.[7]

Income Adjustment and Absolute Advantages

While many economic arguments about competitiveness have focused on exchange rate adjustment, another approach emphasizes the adjustment of national income levels and growth rates. This alternative approach was pioneered by British Keynesian economist A. P. Thirlwall (1979) in his theory of "balance-of-payments constrained growth" (see also Davidson, 1990–91). The income adjustment view has been extended recently by Dosi, Pavitt, and Soete (1990) in their work on "technological gaps" and "absolute competitive advantages." What follows is a brief effort to explain this alternative view of the international adjustment process.

Assuming that countries cannot maintain trade deficits (or surpluses) indefinitely, and that exchange rate adjustments will not necessarily operate, then relative income levels (or growth rates) are constrained in the long run by

The more the U.S. can enhance the competitiveness of its own industries . . . the higher will be the sustainable standard of living.

27

the requirements of balancing trade. The crucial constraints are then the relative intensities of demand for a country's exports and imports, as measured by what economists call "income elasticities."[8] Specifically, if one country (the United States) has a more intense demand for another country's products (say Japan's) than the other country (Japan, in this example) has for their products, then the United States must grow at a slower rate in order to prevent growing trade deficits with Japan. Moreover, this constraint cannot be overcome by macroeconomic policies. On the contrary, macro policy responses designed to cure trade deficits—such as reducing budget deficits—are only likely to reinforce the tendency for slower growth in the less competitive country. Only direct efforts to address problems of relative costs and quality, as well as market access barriers, can overcome this kind of constraint.

The concept of a trade balance constraint on national income implies that the most important question for the United States is not whether it can balance its trade, but *how* to balance its trade. One way to balance trade is to make domestic incomes and expenditures grow sufficiently slowly in order to hold down the growth of imports from the rest of the world. This is the belt-tightening or austerity path, and it will cut domestic living standards just as surely as a continuous real depreciation of the dollar (perhaps even more surely). Yet this is exactly what a reduction in the government budget deficit would accomplish, unless accompanied by other measures to stimulate demand. The alternative is for the United States to adopt industrial and trade policies which can relieve the trade balance constraint, combined with expansionary foreign macro policies and market-opening measures to increase demand for U.S. exports.

The trade balance constraint also helps to explain how industry-level ("microeconomic") competitiveness matters to aggregate ("macroeconomic") performance. Traditionally, economists have maintained that the efficiency of particular national industries only affects the composition of trade, not aggregate trade performance. In the traditional view, industry-level characteristics determine "comparative advantages"—which products a country can produce relatively cheaply, compared with other countries—that determine the pattern of trade—which products a country exports and which ones it imports. Absolute advantages—which country can make particular kinds of goods with

The alternative is for the United States to adopt industrial and trade policies which can relieve the trade balance constraint.

28

greater overall efficiency (less inputs per unit of output)—
are not supposed to matter to the pattern of trade. For
example, the U.S. may have a comparative disadvantage in
textile production even if U.S. textile production is absolutely more efficient than foreign textile production, provided that this productivity advantage in textiles is relatively smaller compared with U.S. advantages in other
sectors (e.g., agriculture).

In their study of *The Economics of Technical Change
and International Trade*, Dosi et al. (1990) concluded that
much international trade in manufactures is determined by
the technological innovativeness of the various national
firms rather than by comparative cost factors. Technological innovation includes the development of new and
improved products as well as more efficient production
processes (which lower costs). Countries with superior
technologies in sectors such as computers, aircraft, chemicals, machinery, and scientific or medical instruments can
export these goods in spite of high wages. The income-
adjustment view says that such absolute technological
advantages determine whether a country will have a tendency to run overall trade surpluses or deficits, and thus
whether it will have a relatively loose or tight trade balance
constraint on its income level and growth rate. The wider
the range of sectors in which a country has such absolute
superiority, the higher are the real wages, per capita
income, and growth rate which are consistent with balanced trade, relative to other countries.

Even in this new view, adjustments of relative wages and
exchange rates can still permit much trade to take place
according to comparative advantages. Thus, for example,
the United States will be a net importer of goods like textiles and steel in which it has lost comparative advantages
(although the more productive and high-end segments of
these domestic industries will remain viable). These same
adjustments also allow countries with superior technologies to have higher real wages and living standards. It is precisely because their wages are higher that these countries
must be net importers of goods in which their absolute productivity advantage is relatively low (i.e., in which they
have a comparative disadvantage). To this extent, the "new
view" agrees with the exchange rate adjustment view discussed earlier.

But the new view adds that there is a second type of
adjustment process, which is the adjustment of relative

*Countries with
superior
technologies in
sectors such as
computers,
aircraft,
chemicals,
machinery, and
scientific or
medical
instruments can
export these
goods in spite of
high wages.*

29

national incomes. A country which has absolute competitive advantages in a wide range of manufacturing industries will be able to grow faster with balanced trade, while a country with absolute competitive disadvantages will have to grow more slowly in order to have balanced trade.[9] Furthermore, there are positive feedbacks from rapid growth and negative feedbacks from slow growth, which tend to reinforce the initial gaps in absolute competitiveness. For example, a rapidly growing country will generally be able to sustain higher rates of saving and investment, and will thus be able to upgrade its capital equipment and raise its productivity faster, while a slowly growing country will generally have low saving and investment rates, and will therefore be saddled with an aging capital stock and sluggish productivity growth. These self-reinforcing mechanisms in international competitiveness are examples of what is called *cumulative causation*—which essentially implies that it is harder for a country to catch up once it has fallen behind.

We shall examine the evidence that the United States is falling behind in absolute competitiveness in Chapters 3 through 5, below. But first we will consider the role of the U.S. government budget deficit and other macro policies in determining the U.S. trade balance.

A rapidly growing country will generally be able to sustain higher rates of saving and investment.

Endnotes

Strictly speaking, the following equation applies to the *current account* balance, which equals the merchandise trade balance plus the services balance (including net inflows of investment income) and net transfers. In this context, the term "trade balance" should be understood to mean the current account.

The definition of macroeconomic stability used here refers to the output adjustment process in the goods market. Assuming that output increases when there is excess demand for goods and decreases when there is excess supply, then output will converge to its equilibrium level if and only if the propensity to save is greater than the propensity to invest out of additional income.

In particular, it is important to have a competitive domestic capital goods sector so that the import coefficient of investment is relatively low.

If a country starts with full capacity utilization or full employment, the effects of a competitive improvement will work through different channels. If it is not possible to increase total output, the composition of domestic output will have to shift toward more production of tradeables and less production of nontradeables. The trade balance may not improve in the short run, especially if the country has to borrow from abroad to finance additional investment in tradeable sectors (including imported capital goods). But total output will eventually increase as new capacity is added. In the long run, the country will probably reach the point where excess capacity eventually reemerges. Then trade surpluses will once again become useful or even necessary for sustaining high employment and incomes. One can view Japan and now Korea as having made this type of transition from economies constrained by capacity limits (and as having achieved export success via labor reallocation to higher-productivity activities) to economies which require trade surpluses to sustain high levels of demand and employment.

Data on industrial capacity utilization are from the U.S. Federal Reserve Board of Governors. Data on unemployment are from the U.S. Department of Labor, Bureau of Labor Statistics.

See Eatwell (1982) and Bazen and Thirlwall (1989) on competitive decline in the British case.

The same point about dynamics applies to the argument of McCulloch and Richardson (1986) and Summers (1988), that an investment-led improvement in competitiveness will cause the trade balance to fall rather than to rise, because the right-hand side of the macro identity (1) will be reduced. An investment-led economic boom has the potential to increase international competitiveness—both by improving product quality and by raising productivity (lowering costs)—especially if the investment is concentrated in internationally competitive sectors such as manufacturing. If this occurs—and it is important to emphasize that this depends on the *composition* of investment, something which is ignored in the traditional aggregative analysis—then the stimulus to net exports and national saving may be great enough to offset the income effect on import demand and to prevent an increase in net borrowing from abroad.

8   The income-elasticity of demand for exports (imports) is the percentage by which demand rises when foreign (domestic) incomes rise by 1 percent. For measures of these elasticities see Table 4 in Chapter 3.

9   Of course, if incomes do not adjust, then persistent trade imbalances will emerge, sustained by international capital movements (lending from surplus countries to deficit countries). This is what has happened to the United States in the last decade.

Chapter 2

Disentangling the Twin Deficits

The analysis in the previous chapter shows that *both* real competitiveness *and* the spending-saving behavior (including fiscal policies) *jointly* determine the trade balance. Nevertheless, macro policies are still important factors which must be taken into account in a complete analysis of the trade balance—especially in regard to the United States, where the Reagan-era tax cuts increased the federal budget deficit dramatically in the early 1980s. The correct question is not if (or to what extent) the budget deficit *per se* causes the trade deficit, but rather how changes in underlying fiscal policies affect both deficits along with private saving and investment.[1] This chapter will seek to answer this question in terms of both economic theory and empirical evidence.

Both real competitiveness and the spending-saving behavior (including fiscal policies) jointly determine the trade balance.

Twin Deficit Connections

Figure 1 illustrates some of the most common stories which are told about the "twin deficits." The most direct effect of expansionary fiscal policy (mostly tax cuts, in this case) is to pump up domestic expenditures and thus to increase demand for imports. Assuming that foreign demand for U.S. exports remains unchanged, the result is an increased trade deficit matching the reduction in "national savings" according to the macro identity (1).

Expansionary fiscal policy can also have indirect effects on the trade balance via induced changes in the value of the dollar. According to this argument, government borrowing to finance its deficit spending puts upward pressure on interest rates. As U.S. interest rates rise relative to foreign interest rates, foreign funds flow into U.S. financial assets. The increased demand for dollars to buy U.S. financial assets drives up the value of the dollar.[2] Then the higher value of the dollar makes U.S. products (both exported and import-competing goods) less competitive, resulting in a rise in the trade deficit. This argument has been applied to the 1980–85 period by Dornbusch (1985), Feldstein (1986), and Marris (1985), among others.

Some economists argue that in fact trade (current account) deficits today are really just artifacts of net capital inflows.

Since, as we have seen, international capital movements dwarf international trade transactions, some economists argue that in fact trade (current account) deficits today are really just artifacts of net capital inflows (borrowing from abroad). A country would be expected to have positive net capital inflows (a capital account surplus) when rates of return on domestic assets (including interest rates on bonds) exceed rates of return on comparable foreign assets (corrected for expected exchange rate changes). Then the rising U.S. trade deficit in the 1980s can be explained as the result of an increase in the rate of return on U.S. assets relative to foreign assets (see McCulloch and Richardson,

Figure 1
Twin Deficit Connections:
The Conventional Wisdom

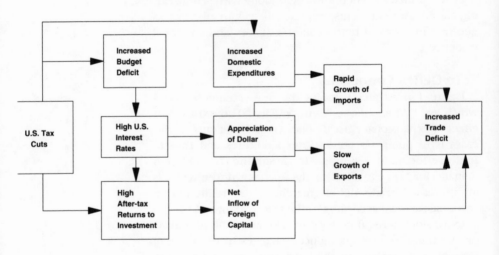

1986). This provides another channel through which changes in fiscal policies can affect the trade balance, as shown at the bottom of Figure 1: tax cuts raise the after-tax returns on U.S. investments, while also raising before-tax interest rates for the reasons discussed earlier. This contributes to the appreciation of the dollar as well as to our ability to finance net imports of goods and services (the trade deficit).

All these "twin deficit" stories are plausible and contain important elements of truth. But these stories are as notable for what they omit as for what they say. Even if we leave aside issues of competitiveness, these stories ignore other macro policies which also influence both the value of the dollar and the trade balance: foreign fiscal policies, and both domestic and foreign monetary policies. The prediction of increased net imports (a rising trade deficit) need not hold if foreign countries simultaneously conduct expansionary fiscal policies, which would stimulate their demand for U.S. exports at the same time as the United States stimulates its demand for their exports. And the prediction of a rising dollar need not hold if U.S. monetary policy reacts by accommodating the rising government budget deficits and holding interest rates down.

> *All these "twin deficit" stories . . . ignore other macro policies which also influence both the value of the dollar and the trade balance.*

Figure 2 tries to fill in some of the gaps in the conventional twin deficit stories by illustrating the complex interdependencies which link the trade and budget deficits to each other, to other macroeconomic variables, and to structural conditions. This broader view of the connection does allow for expansionary fiscal policies to raise the trade deficit through increased domestic expenditures, but it places more emphasis on tight monetary policy in raising interest rates and causing the dollar to appreciate. Figure 2 also shows the direct impact of competitive decline and foreign market barriers on trade flows, as well as the negative effect of contractionary foreign macro policies on export growth.

Figure 2 also illustrates some of the feedback effects which operate to exacerbate both the budget and trade deficits. One of these effects is the increased government debt service resulting from deficit spending itself, along with the high interest rates on the debt caused by tight monetary policy. Another feedback effect is the loss of tax revenue due to the slower growth of national income which is caused by the trade deficit; the loss of tax revenue in turn worsens the budget deficit and thus reduces national saving. Finally, Figure 2 shows the possibility that an overvalued dollar could aggravate the structural decline in competitiveness (this last point will be explained later in this chapter).

It should be expected that there will be some spillover of expansionary fiscal policy changes into a foreign trade deficit, holding all these other factors constant.[3] To understand why, it is helpful to rewrite the national income identity (2) in the form:

(3)   Government Deficit =
       Private Saving − Domestic Investment
                    + Net Foreign Saving

where net foreign saving equals the current account *deficit*. There are thus *three* ways in which an increased government deficit must ultimately finance itself: a rise in private saving, a fall in domestic investment, or a rise in net foreign saving (fall in the trade balance). We shall focus our attention on private and foreign saving, since there is little evidence for domestic investment having been "crowded out" in the 1980s.[4]

*It should be
expected that
there will be
some spillover of
expansionary
fiscal policy
changes into a
foreign trade
deficit.*

Figure 2
The Trade and Budget Deficits:
A Broader View

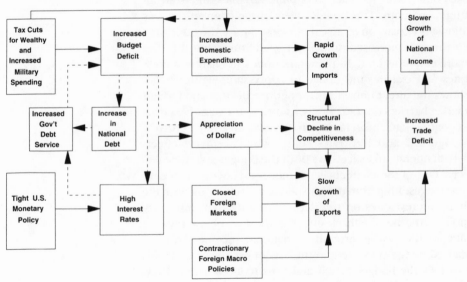

Note: Dashed lines represent feedback effects and weaker relationships.

36

Although the conventional wisdom views government deficits strictly as subtracting from total "national saving," in fact expansionary fiscal policy can have a positive effect on private saving. Fiscal expansion will raise private saving provided that there are unemployed resources (labor and capital equipment) which can be brought into production by increasing aggregate demand. In this situation, deficit spending stimulates more output and employment, thus generating higher incomes for workers, firms, and investors. As part of these increased incomes is saved, private saving also rises relative to what it would be otherwise. In particular, corporate profits should increase, leading to a rise in corporate saving.

In fact expansionary fiscal policy can have a positive effect on private saving.

In an economy which is open to foreign trade, however, a portion of the increased national income will be spent on imported goods and services. Increased demand for imports stimulates output and employment in foreign countries, generating increased incomes abroad. Part of those increased incomes then flow back into the home country in the form of capital inflows (net foreign savings) equal to the rise in the trade deficit. The additional net foreign savings which flow into the home country must exactly equal the increased net imports of goods and services. Thus the fact that expansionary fiscal policy can lead to increased net foreign savings (a higher trade deficit) can be seen as a generalization of the basic Keynesian principle that deficit spending finances itself by increasing saving— the only difference is that in this case it is foreign rather than domestic saving that increases. In this sense, deficit spending does not deplete global private savings; indeed, it will generally increase them, as long as there are excess capacity and unemployed workers abroad.

It is precisely for this reason that it is crucial to take account of how other countries' fiscal policies are changing when the home country pursues expansionary policies. If all countries expand simultaneously, the negative effects on each country's trade balance will roughly cancel out as all nations import more from each other. In this case, no significant increase in trade imbalances should be expected. On the other hand, if foreign countries happen to tighten their fiscal policies at the same time as the home country expands, then the resulting global imbalances will surely be worse. In this case, the home country will experience a rise in its trade deficit beyond what is necessary to finance its own budget deficit, as foreign demand for exports will fall off. Furthermore, the reduction in export demand will have negative effects on national saving (both private saving and the budget balance), analogous to the effects of a competitive decline discussed in the previous chapter. This would create the appearance of a "twin deficit" relationship in the home country, without domestic fiscal policies being fully responsible. In this situation, domestic deficits are indeed the "engine of global growth," but only because foreign governments are keeping their locomotives in the roundhouse.

Global Imbalances and the U.S. Deficits

The importance of foreign macro policies for exacerbating the U.S. trade deficit in the early 1980s can be seen from the data in Table 1. This table compares the changes in the current account, saving-investment, and budget balances between 1974–79 and 1980–87 in the United States and the two largest industrialized surplus nations, Japan and West Germany.[5] While the U.S. government surplus fell by 1.9 percent of gross domestic product (GDP), the Japanese government surplus rose by 1.0 percent of GDP, and the West German surplus rose by 0.4 percent. *It was this opposite movement in fiscal policies which led to such massive trade imbalances,* especially with Japan, not the increased U.S. fiscal deficit alone.

In fact, U.S. fiscal expansion in the early 1980s made it possible for Japan, and to a lesser extent West Germany, to tighten their budgets without suffering aggregate demand problems, as their growing external surpluses (mainly with the U.S.) substituted for domestic demand. At the same time, the reduction in foreign demand worsened the U.S. trade balance, and simultaneously reduced U.S. national income and saving (including the government budget surplus) relative to what they would have been otherwise. Thus the fact that the changes in the U.S. current account and budget balances are of similar magnitude (− 1.8 and − 1.9 percent, respectively) does not necessarily confirm the "twin deficit" view that U.S. fiscal policy caused all or most of the U.S. trade deficit. At least to some extent, lower foreign demand caused both balances to fall.

With regard to private saving behavior, the data in Table 1 refute the common assertion that part of the U.S. trade deficit may be attributed to the falling U.S. *private* saving rate.[6] Although the U.S. saving rate is evidently much lower than the German and Japanese saving rates, by far the largest

> It was this opposite movement in fiscal policies which led to such massive trade imbalances, especially with Japan, not the increased U.S. fiscal deficit alone.

TABLE 1
Current Account, Saving-Investment, and Budget Balances for the United States, Japan, and West Germany, 1974–79 to 1980–87
(in percent of GDP)

Country	Period	Current Account	=	Gross Private Saving[a]	−	Gross Domestic Investment[b]	+	Government Budget Surplus[c]	+	Statistical Discrepancy[d]
U.S.	1974–79	0.3		19.7		(17.7)		−1.8		0.1
	1980–87	−1.6		18.9		(16.8)		−3.7		0.0
	Change[e]	−1.8		−0.8		(−0.8)		−1.9		+0.1
Japan	1974–79	0.3		29.4		(27.1)		−2.2		0.2
	1980–87	2.1		27.0		(24.1)		−1.2		0.4
	Change[e]	+1.7		−2.5		(−3.0)		+1.0		+0.2
Germany	1974–79	1.0		20.2		(18.0)		−1.2		0.0
	1980–87	1.3		20.0		(17.9)		−0.8		0.0
	Change[e]	+0.3		−0.1		(−0.1)		+0.4		−0.1

Source: OECD, *National Accounts, Volume II, Detailed Tables, 1974–1987* (Paris, 1989), and author's calculations.

Notes:
[a]Sum of net national saving plus consumption of fixed capital (including public corporations, but excluding general government).
[b]Gross fixed capital formation (including public corporations, but excluding general government) plus increase in stocks.
[c]General government net saving plus depreciation allowances minus fixed capital formation (excluding public corporations).
[d]Includes rounding error.
[e]Equals 1980–87 average minus 1974–79 average. Changes were rounded separately.

decline in saving rates between 1974–79 and 1980–87 was the 2.5 percent of GDP drop recorded in Japan. Holding other factors constant, the greater reduction in the Japanese private saving rates by itself should have *improved* the U.S. bilateral trade balance with Japan. But the even larger drop in the Japanese investment rate[7] (3.0 percent of GDP) more than offset the fall in the Japanese saving rate (2.5 percent of GDP), and thus further increased Japan's net outflow of savings (trade surplus).

In any case, no matter how much fiscal policies and other macroeconomic variables (including exchange rates) can explain the *rise* in the U.S. trade deficit in the early 1980s (and we shall see below that they can explain only part of that rise), they clearly cannot explain most of the *persistence* of large trade deficits in the late 1980s and the early 1990s. For one thing, the dollar peaked in value in 1985 and had returned to about its 1980 value by the end of the decade. Therefore, any explanation which rests on fiscal deficits causing appreciation of the dollar cannot be applied to the more recent period. And macro policies in most other countries did become more expansionary in the late 1980s, thus eliminating the discrepancy between U.S. and foreign demand which grew at similar rates over the 1980s as a whole.

To illustrate this point, Table 2 shows how U.S. and foreign incomes and the real value of the dollar changed between 1980, 1985, and 1990.[8] In 1985, U.S. income (measured by GDP) had risen 15 percent over its 1980 level (in constant dollars). This was almost double the growth experienced in Europe from 1980–85 (8 percent), but less than the growth in Japan and the developing countries. All other industrial countries (Europe and Japan plus Canada, Australia, and New Zealand) together grew about four-fifths as fast as the U.S. (12 versus 15 percent) in those years. Also, by 1985, the dollar had increased somewhere between 35 and 56 percent in real value (on a trade-weighted basis, correcting for different inflation rates at home and abroad), depending on the particular index used. Thus, the macro factors which would tend to raise the U.S. trade deficit—faster income growth at home combined with an appreciation of the dollar—were indeed found in the 1980–85 period.

By 1990, however, these macro factors were almost entirely reversed. European growth recovered, and was slightly more rapid than American growth in the

> No matter how much fiscal policies and other macroeconomic variables . . . can explain the rise in the U.S. trade deficit in the early 1980s . . . they clearly cannot explain most of the persistence of large trade deficits in the late 1980s. . . .

TABLE 2
Macroeconomic Determinants of U.S. Trade Balance
1980, 1985, and 1990

(All variables measured as index numbers, 1980 = 100,
except as noted)

	1980	1985	1990
National Incomes			
United States[a]	100	115	133
Other Industrial Countries[a,b]	100	112	133
Western Europe	100	108	126
Japan	100	121	153
Developing Countries[c]	100	116	137
Real Exchange Rates (Value of Dollar)			
FRB G-10 Real Index[d,e]	100	156	102
Dallas Fed 101 Countries Index[e,f]	100	135	110
IMF Wholesale Price Index[g]	100	136	95
IMF Unit Labor Cost Index[g]	100	138	75
Trade Balance			
Merchandise[h]	−12	−136	−93
Nonoil, nonagricatural[h]	32	−106	−38
Current Account[i]	13	−114	−86

Notes:

[a]Measured by gross domestic products (GDP) in constant 1985 dollars. From Organisation for Economic Co-operation and Development (OECD), *Main Economic Indicators,* February 1991, p. 172.

[b]Total OECD minus U.S. and Turkey. Includes some countries not listed separately (Canada, Australia, New Zealand).

[c]From index in International Monetary Fund, *International Financial Statistics,* 1990 Yearbook, p. 165. Index extrapolated to 1990 at average annual rate for 1980–88.

[d]From *Economic Report of the President,* 1991, p. 410, based on data from Board of Governors of the Federal Reserve System.

[e]Nominal exchange rates are adjusted by consumer price indexes.

[f]Unpublished data from Federal Reserve Bank of Dallas.

[g]From IMF, *International Financial Statistics, 1990 Yearbook,* pp. 110–11, and May 1991, pp. 66–67.

[h]National Income and Product Accounts basis, in billions of constant 1982 dollars. Revised 1990 data from U.S. Department of Commerce, *Survey of Current Business,* April 1991.

[i]Net foreign investment, National Income and Product Accounts basis, in billions of current dollars.

1985–1990 period, while Japanese growth continued to be robust. As a result, by 1990, other industrial countries had grown just as much as the United States (33 percent), relative to 1980, while developing countries continued to grow even faster (37 percent over the whole decade). Moreover, the 1980–85 rise in the dollar was completely reversed in 1985–1990 by most of the measures shown, and mostly reversed by the other measure (the Dallas Fed real index for 101 countries).[9] Yet in 1990, the merchandise trade balance (in constant 1982 dollars) was $81 billion lower than in 1980; excluding oil imports and agricultural exports, the merchandise balance was $70 billion lower. And the current account balance was $99 billion lower (in current dollars).[10] These persistent reductions in various measures of the trade balance cannot be attributed to differences in U.S. and foreign macro policies or to changes in exchange rates, and must instead be presumed to reflect structural factors.

Monetary Policy and the Dollar

Since monetary policy played an active and independent role in the 1980s, it is worth briefly reviewing the shifts in U.S. monetary policy before turning to their effects on trade.[11] A dramatic move toward tighter monetary policy occurred *before* the shift to more expansionary fiscal policies took place in 1981–83. Beginning in October 1979, under new Chairman Paul Volcker, the Federal Reserve Bank used tight monetary policies and high interest rates as weapons in the battle to control inflation, as well as to arrest the 1978–79 fall in the value of the dollar. As the Fed's "credible" commitment to anti-inflationary policies restored confidence in financial markets, and as higher U.S. interest rates attracted funds back into U.S. assets, the dollar stabilized in 1980 and rose in 1981, as shown in Figure 3. This initial upturn in the dollar came *before* most of the Reagan income tax cuts took effect in 1982 and 1983, and *before* the biggest increases in the federal deficit.[12]

In spite of its new "operating procedures" which targeted the money supply, the Fed was unable to generate the smooth, slow growth of the money supply advocated by monetarists. Whenever the Fed tried to tighten, interest rates soared to astronomical levels. The prime rate on bank loans reached as high as 20 percent several times in 1980–81. The result was two back-to-back recessions (one in early 1980 and the other in 1981–82), the second one the most severe since the Great Depression of the 1930s.

> *A dramatic move toward tighter monetary policy occurred before the shift to more expansionary fiscal policies took place in 1981–83.*

Figure 3
Weighted Average Exchange Value of the U.S. Dollar, Quarterly 1967-1990

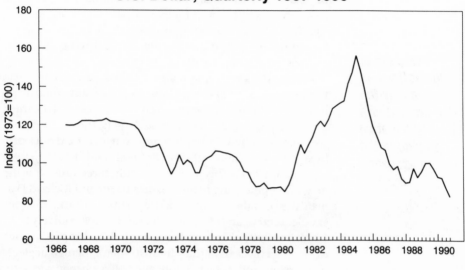

Source: Federal Reserve Board of Governors.
Note: Official index based on 1972-76 world trade weights for 10 industrial country currencies.

Each time, the Fed had to reverse course and ease credit conditions temporarily in order to end the recession and permit recovery. The 1982 recession was so serious as to threaten a financial crisis, as Latin American nations announced they could no longer service their foreign debts, and many domestic financial institutions were in danger of failure (see Wolfson, 1986; Greider, 1987). The Fed responded by temporarily abandoning its tight policies in late 1982 and early 1983, pumping enough monetary reserves into the banks to prevent a financial collapse.

This was the monetary policy environment in which Reagan's tax cuts under the Economic Recovery Tax Act (ERTA) of 1981 took effect, phased in over a three-year period. The tax cuts, together with the temporary relaxation of monetary policy, contributed to a relatively strong cyclical recovery—albeit from a very depressed base—in 1983. But by the end of that year, and again in 1984, the Fed returned to tight monetary policy out of fear of renewed inflation during the recovery then underway. Thus, when the final Reagan tax cuts took effect, and at the same time that military outlays were accelerating, these

43

expansionary fiscal shifts were accompanied by the slowest monetary growth in recent history.[13] Interest rates went back up slightly in nominal terms in 1984, but much more in real terms as inflationary expectations were reduced (see Figure 4 and Table 3 for estimated real interest rates). A significant real interest rate differential in favor of the United States opened up (see Figure 5), driving the dollar further up in 1984 (Frankel, 1985).

By late 1984 and early 1985, however, the dollar began to rise far more than could be explained by any "fundamentals" such as interest rate differentials. As discussed earlier, the final peak of the dollar was largely the product of a speculative bubble in the foreign exchange market (Dornbusch, 1988a and 1989b; Frankel and Froot, 1990; Krugman, 1989). This bubble was punctured only after the new, more pragmatic team of James Baker and Richard Darman was installed at the U.S. Department of the Treasury (as Secretary and Deputy Secretary, respectively). As Frankel (1990) observed, this event led market participants to expect a reversal of the administration's "benign neglect" of the rising dollar, even before any policy change was actu-

> *The final peak of the dollar was largely the product of a speculative bubble in the foreign exchange market.*

Figure 4
Real Interest Rates in the United States,
Quarterly 1960-1990

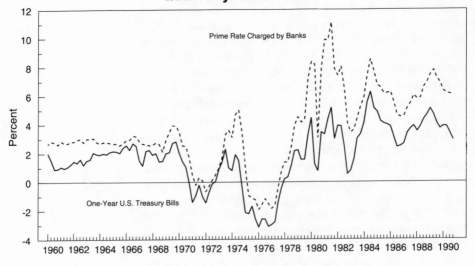

Sources: Federal Reserve Board of Governors and Department of Commerce, BEA.
Note: The expected inflation rate is measured as the average increase in the GNP deflator for the past 12 quarters.

44

TABLE 3
U.S. Real Interest Rates, Decade Averages, 1960–1989
(in percent)

Years	One-Year Treasury Bill	Prime Rate Charged by Banks	Moody's AAA Bond Rate
1960–69	1.8%	2.9%	2.6%
1970–79	−0.2	1.4	1.5
1980–89	3.6	6.5	6.0

Sources: U.S. Federal Reserve Board of Governors; U.S. Department of Commerce, BEA, National Income and Product Accounts; and author's calculations.

Note: Real interest rates were calculated by subtracting an estimate of the expected inflation rate from the average nominal interest rate for each quarter. Expected inflation was estimated by the average rate of increase in the GNP deflator over the preceding 12 quarters (3 years).

Figure 5
U.S.-German Real Interest Rate Differential on Treasury Bills, Annual Averages 1980-1990

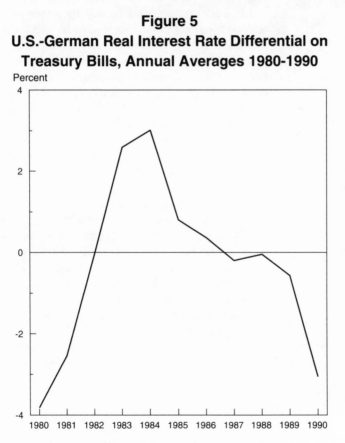

Sources: IMF, International Financial Statistics; Federal Reserve
Board of Governors; and author's calculations.
Note: Inflation rates averaged for current and previous year.

45

ally announced. In addition, the German monetary authorities intervened to stop the dollar's appreciation in February and March of 1985, after getting approval at a G-5 meeting in London in January. It was not until September 1985, after the dollar had been falling for six months, that the G-5 finance ministers issued their famous announcement at the Plaza Hotel which confirmed their commitment to see the dollar fall further.

> **The rise of the dollar in the early 1980s resulted from the combination of fiscal expansion with monetary contraction, not from the fiscal expansion by itself.**

In order to validate this commitment, the Fed was forced to allow the U.S. money supply to grow at record rates in 1985–86.[14] As a result, real interest rates fell and the dollar came down, bottoming out in 1987–88, when international central bank intervention combined with U.S. monetary tightening halted the dollar's decline. These gyrations in the foreign exchange market in 1985–88 were mainly driven by monetary policies, central bank interventions, and the actions of foreign exchange speculators. Although the U.S. government did reduce its structural (cyclically-adjusted) budget deficit somewhat in 1987–88, this came *two years after* the dollar began to fall.

This brief review of the events of the 1980s should suffice to call into question part of the twin deficit connection depicted in Figure 1: the chain of causality which runs from an increased budget deficit through higher interest rates to the appreciation of the dollar. At a minimum, we can see that the rise of the dollar in the early 1980s resulted from the *combination* of fiscal expansion with monetary contraction, not from the fiscal expansion by itself. Indeed, the fact that these two types of macro policies went hand-in-hand makes it difficult to separate out their respective contributions to the rise in the dollar. This probably explains why estimates of these separate effects vary widely, and seem to depend mainly on the assumptions built into the economic models used to derive the estimates (see Bryant et al., 1988). For what it is worth, however, a mid-range estimate is that only about one-fifth of the dollar's rise in 1980–85 can be attributed to the U.S. fiscal expansion, holding monetary policy and other factors constant.[15] This would imply that dollar appreciation was a relatively minor channel for the transmission of expansionary fiscal policy into a rising trade deficit.

Effects of the Overvalued Dollar

There is an important distinction between the effects of monetary policy on the dollar and on the trade deficit. The

46

immediate effect of a tight monetary policy is to raise interest rates. But higher interest rates have two offsetting effects on the trade balance. On the one hand, higher interest rates cause the dollar to appreciate, thus making American products less competitive, which tends to worsen the trade balance. On the other hand, higher interest rates depress domestic spending and reduce import demand, which tends to improve the trade balance. Thus the net effect of tight monetary policy on the trade balance is ambiguous, and depends on which of these effects is stronger.

Declining price competitiveness due to the rising value of the dollar accounted for most of the increased merchandise trade deficit in the first half of the 1980s.

For this reason, a number of economists (including Sachs, 1988, and Helkie and Hooper, 1988) have argued that the tight monetary policies of the 1980s were not a major independent cause of the increased U.S. trade deficit. Rather, the tight monetary policies altered the *form* which the trade deficit took in the early 1980s. As Hooper stated elsewhere, "Monetary policy had little net effect on its own, though it did *increase the contribution of exchange rate movements and reduce the importance of relative incomes* to the widening of the external deficit" (1989, p. 38, italics added). That is, the negative income effects of monetary contraction partly offset the positive income effects of fiscal expansion, while the monetary contraction increased the appreciation of the dollar in 1980–85.

This view is supported by evidence that declining price competitiveness due to the rising value of the dollar accounted for most of the increased merchandise trade deficit in the first half of the 1980s. For example, Helkie and Hooper (1988) find much greater effects of relative price (real exchange rate) changes than relative income shifts for explaining trends in U.S. trade in the 1980s. From 1980 to 1986, the U.S. merchandise trade deficit (excluding agricultural exports and oil imports) rose by $165 billion.[16] Out of this total, $121 billion, or nearly three-quarters, is attributed by Helkie and Hooper to relative price changes, only $18 billion to relative income changes, and $26 billion is attributed to changes in "relative supply."[17]

Helkie and Hooper argue that if monetary policy had been less restrictive, the price effects would have been smaller and the income effects larger, but the total rise in the trade deficit would have been about the same. As noted earlier, it is probably impossible to reach any firm conclusion on the independent effect of monetary policy on the trade deficit. But even if it were true that monetary policy had a relatively small net impact on the trade deficit, this would not necessarily imply that monetary policy was benign in its effects on underlying U.S. competitiveness.

To say that tight monetary policy in the 1980s merely shifted the source of the trade deficit from relative income effects to relative price effects is to miss an important implication. If a trade deficit results simply from domestic demand stimulus—as in the case of a fiscal deficit accommodated by monetary expansion—then the trade deficit will be due mainly to the income effects of the fiscal deficit on import demand. Neither export producers nor import-competing firms need suffer in this case, as imports just grow along with the domestic market. But if a trade deficit results from overvaluation of the currency due to excessive monetary contraction, then the trade deficit is due mainly to a loss of price competitiveness, and *this adversely affects both export producers and import-competing firms who would otherwise be able to compete effectively.* Thus the devastating consequences of the overvalued dollar of the mid-1980s on such sectors as agriculture and capital goods—both of which are relatively efficient and intrinsically competitive—must be attributed to the Fed's monetary policy, not to the government's budget deficit.

Moreover, the anticompetitive effects of an overvalued dollar can persist even after the dollar eventually falls. This idea of *permanent* or *irreversible* effects of a temporary exchange rate change has become known as "hysteresis." In particular, it has been argued that the dollar overvaluation of the mid-1980s may have had lasting negative effects on U.S. competitiveness, especially in import-competing sectors.

One interesting theory of hysteresis is Baldwin's (1988) model of the "beachhead effect." In this model, a temporary but large appreciation of a nation's currency induces foreign firms to enter the domestic market, by making it worthwhile for them to pay the fixed, sunk costs of market entry (e.g., establishing a distribution network). Even if the currency eventually returns to its previous value, the foreign firms remain in the domestic market as long as they can still make a profit over their operating costs in their own currency in spite of the home currency's depreciation. Thus the market structure of the home country is permanently altered by a transitory overvaluation of its currency: the market share of imports is higher after the currency returns to its original value than it was before the currency initially appreciated.

> *If a trade deficit results from overvaluation of the currency . . . this adversely affects both export producers and import-competing firms who would otherwise be able to compete effectively.*

Other forms of hysteresis are conceivable. By analogy with Baldwin's model, national firms could shift production overseas during the period of overvaluation, paying the fixed, sunk costs of relocation while they are low in terms of the home currency. Then, after the home currency depreciates, those firms can maintain foreign production as long as the operating costs abroad, converted to domestic currency, remain low enough to allow for profitable export back to the home country. In some product lines, little or no domestic production may remain after the overvaluation is reversed.

Econometric Studies: Twins or Cousins?

A number of studies have attempted to quantify the "twin deficit" relationship by estimating how much the increased budget deficit contributed to the increased trade deficit in the early 1980s. Not surprisingly, the estimates vary greatly. A systematic comparison of international macroeconomic models conducted by Bryant et al. (1988) revealed that different models constructed according to different assumptions about how the economy works yield very different quantitative (and sometimes even qualitative) results about the effects of shifts in fiscal policies, monetary policies, and exchange rates. For example, while most of the models in the study agree that a 1 percent of GNP fiscal stimulus in the United States would lower the current account balance, estimates of the magnitude of this effect (cumulated over 6 years) range from $3 billion to $53 billion. And the models are split roughly in half on whether a monetary stimulus will improve or worsen the current account, either in the short- or medium-run (1 to 6 years).

The model which generated the *largest* estimated effect of fiscal expansion on the trade deficit in the Bryant et al. study was the Multicountry Model (MCM) of the Federal Reserve Board. Helkie and Hooper (1988, p. 48) applied this model to analyze the underlying macroeconomic causes of the increased U.S. current account deficit from 1980 to 1986.[18] They estimated that U.S. fiscal expansion accounted for about a $70 billion rise in the current account deficit, or just under half of the actual increase of $143 billion, holding domestic monetary and foreign fiscal policies constant. In addition, they estimate that "foreign fiscal contraction contributed another $25 billion to the deficit," so that domestic and foreign fiscal policies combined explain a total of $95 billion of the increased current deficit, or about two-thirds

A high-end estimate of the "twin deficit" relationship is that less than half of the 1980–87 rise in the trade deficit can be explained by the rise in the U.S. budget deficit!

49

of the total increase (Helkie and Hooper, 1988, p. 49).[19] Thus a *high-end* estimate of the "twin deficit" relationship is that *less than half* of the 1980–87 rise in the trade deficit can be explained by the rise in the U.S. budget deficit! And most of the other macro models surveyed by Bryant et al. (1988) yield substantially *smaller* estimates of this relationship. As Hooper concluded elsewhere,

> Fiscal policy, or the twin deficit relationship, is a significant part of the story, but evidently explains *no more than half* of the decline in our net foreign saving [i.e., current account balance]. The remaining half must be explained by fundamentals other than macroeconomic policy that led to a decline in private domestic saving relative to investment. (1989, p. 38, italics added)

In another important empirical study of international imbalances, Sachs (1988, p. 645) found that "a sustained, bond-financed U.S. fiscal expansion (an increase in federal spending on goods and services [of 1 percent of GNP]) . . . worsens the U.S. trade [current account] balance . . . by an average of 0.31 percent of GNP over three years." Although Sachs' result is obtained from simulations of a large-scale general equilibrium model of the world economy (the McKibbin-Sachs Global Model—see McKibbin and Sachs, 1989), an almost identical result is obtained in a much simpler econometric exercise by Bernheim (1988). Using a single equation model in which only the budget deficit and the GNP growth rate (current and lagged) are used to explain the current account, Bernheim finds that "a $1 increase in government budget deficits leads to roughly a $0.30 rise in the current account deficit" (p. 2) in the United States. Sachs' and Bernheim's results imply that a $100 billion reduction in the budget deficit would eliminate only about $30 billion of the current account deficit— even assuming an offsetting monetary expansion, as Sachs does.

On this basis, Sachs concluded that,

> The U.S. fiscal expansion was only *one* of the reasons for the widening of the U.S. current account deficit. Completely *eliminating* the U.S. budget deficit, other things being equal, would remove no more than half the current external gap. . . . Balancing the U.S. current account will therefore require policy actions or other economic events . . . beyond balancing the U.S. budget. (Sachs, 1988, pp. 646–47; italics in original)

A $100 billion reduction in the budget deficit would eliminate only about $30 billion of the current account deficit.

Sachs' model simulations imply that cutting the budget deficit by 3.8 percent of GNP over five years (together with an accommodating reversal of monetary policy) "reduces the U.S. trade deficit relative to baseline ... by [a cumulative] 1.3 percent of GNP by the fifth year. The 3.8 percentage point phased reduction in fiscal deficits... does not come close to eliminating the trade deficit, which starts at 3.4 percent of GNP in 1986" (Sachs, 1988, pp. 662–63).

The Missing Link: Income Distribution

Given the relatively small estimates of the twin deficit relationship, one might wonder why economists have devoted so much attention to this cause of the trade deficit to the exclusion of other causes. The motivation for this emphasis lies in the theoretical biases which most (though not all) economists bring to the subject. The dominant theoretical paradigm in economics today is the "neoclassical" approach. According to this paradigm, budget deficits are pernicious because they deplete national saving and thus impoverish future generations:

> The Neoclassical paradigm envisions farsighted individuals planning consumption over their own life cycles. Budget deficits raise total lifetime consumption [for the present generation] by shifting taxes to subsequent generations. If economic resources are fully employed, increased consumption necessarily implies decreased saving. Interest rates must then rise to bring capital markets into balance. Thus, persistent [fiscal] deficits "crowd out" private capital accumulation. (Bernheim, 1989, p. 55)

It may be noted that this approach rests on the assumption that "economic resources are fully employed," which we have argued is unrealistic. Ironically, full employment has rarely occurred in the modern U.S. economy *without* large budget deficits to sustain aggregate demand![20] But what is perhaps more notable in this approach is the exclusive focus on the "intertemporal" and "intergenerational" redistributive effects of budget deficits. That is, budget deficits are seen as transferring income from future time periods and future generations to the present. Although in a closed economy this transfer would take the form of reduced investment, in an open economy it can take the form of a trade deficit which implies a growing net foreign debt. Thus neoclassical economists are led to the twin defi-

Given the relatively small estimates of the twin deficit relationship, one might wonder why economists have devoted so much attention to [it]. . . .

51

cits perspective in which budget deficits crowd out net exports instead of domestic investment (Dornbusch, 1985), and future generations are impoverished by a large net foreign debt as well as eventual higher taxes.

This obsession with the intergenerational effects of budget deficits has led neoclassical economists to a stunning neglect of the *contemporaneous* (*intra*generational) redistributive effects of the 1980s fiscal policies. The fiscal policy changes which produced widening federal deficits in the early 1980s ended up almost exclusively benefiting the richest 10 percent of households, and a very large portion of the benefits went to the richest 1 percent (Pechman, 1990; McIntyre, 1990). Moreover, the payment of high rates of interest on a growing national debt largely redistributed income from middle-class taxpayers to wealthy bondholders (Michl, 1991). Thus most of the population utterly failed to participate in the supposed consumption binge of the present generation. At the same time, it appears that the wealthy did go on a consumption binge in the 1980s, spending a large percentage of the extra income they received from tax cuts, high interest rates, and corporate mergers and acquisitions (see Blecker, 1990a, 1991a).

In fact, some of what appear to have been effects of *expansionary* fiscal policies were in fact effects of the more *regressive* structure of the tax system in the past decade, along with changes in the financial behavior of corporations.[21] The federal budget deficit rose most sharply in 1983, when it first crossed the $200 billion threshold. This was the year of the initial recovery from the 1982 recession. But this recovery was not like any previous postwar cyclical recovery.

As in previous cyclical recoveries, the share of capital income (profits and interest) in total national income rose between 1982 and 1984. In previous recoveries, the rising share of capital income always led to a rise in the national saving rate, as personal capital income (interest and dividends) was concentrated in the upper-income households which tended to save more and to be taxed at higher rates. In addition, corporations could be counted on to save a large portion of their profits as retained earnings which were reinvested. But in 1983–84, the national saving rate never recovered. One reason was that the marginal tax rates on upper-income households had been greatly reduced. In addition, the boom in asset markets (e.g., stocks and real estate) combined with high interest rates led

> *The fiscal policy changes which produced widening federal deficits in the early 1980s ended up almost exclusively benefiting the richest 10 percent of households.*

wealthy households to spend more out of current income rather than to save as much as they used to, while marginal tax rates on capital gains had been cut. And corporations began to pay out more of their cash flow to households, mainly in the form of net interest payments on debts incurred for merger and acquisition activity, as well as in the form of stock repurchases, thus reducing their effective reinvestment rate (Blair and Litan, 1990). All of these factors contributed to the fall in the national saving rate which was the flip side of the increased current account deficit in the mid-1980s.

The point of this discussion is not to deny that there are any links between the budget deficit, the low national saving rate, and the trade deficit, but to suggest that these links are considerably more complex than they appear in the conventional (neoclassical) story. The fiscal policy changes of the 1980s affected the distribution of income not only between future generations and the present, but also between different income groups in the present—largely favoring the very wealthy at the expense of the rest of the population. And changes in the financial structure associated with the speculative frenzy of the mid-1980s appear to have had a negative effect on the private saving propensity out of current income, especially for corporations, stockholders, and bondholders. These changes in both public policy and private behavior must be taken into account in formulating macroeconomic and financial policies for the 1990s. Certainly, there are no grounds for the view that tax increases or spending cuts which would fall primarily on working-class and middle-class families have to be accepted in order to curb "overconsumption" and to reduce the "twin deficits." Rather, restoring the progressivity of the income tax system and placing some limits on financial speculation (e.g., through an asset turnover tax) would make more sense for reversing the macroeconomic trends which have contributed, to whatever extent, to worsening the trade deficit.

Restoring the progressivity of the income tax system and placing some limits on financial speculation . . . would make more sense for reversing the macroeconomic trends which have contributed, to whatever extent, to worsening the trade deficit.

Endnotes

1   I am indebted to Ron Blackwell for emphasizing this point.

2   A more sophisticated version of this argument, based on the theory of Dornbusch (1976), argues that the dollar must "overshoot" in the upward direction when U.S. interest rates exceed foreign rates. This creates the expectation of a future decline in the dollar and thus makes the expected returns to U.S. assets (the interest rate minus the expected percentage depreciation of the dollar) equal the expected returns to foreign assets (the foreign interest rate). See Branson (1985) for an application of this theory.

3   The discussion which follows draws upon Blecker (1991a).

4   The monetarist doctrine of "crowding out" assumes that the central bank refuses to accommodate the fiscal deficit and thus raises interest rates. But in an open economy with a high degree of international capital mobility, higher interest rates lead to currency appreciation which lowers net exports rather than domestic investment. Also, in an economy which starts with high unemployment and excess capacity (as the U.S. economy did in the early 1980s), expansionary fiscal policy can potentially "crowd in" investment by making demand grow faster and raising corporate profits, both of which tend to stimulate more investment in spite of higher interest rates (see Eisner, 1978 and 1989; Taylor, 1985).

Empirically, the share of gross investment expenditures in U.S. GNP was not unusually low (or high) in the 1980s, although some other measures of the investment rate give different impressions. See Blecker (1990a) for more details.

5   The table focuses on the period up to 1987 which is when the U.S. trade deficit peaked. The role of contractionary macro policies in the developing countries, especially the Latin American debtors, will be discussed in Chapter 6.

6   For critical perspectives on the view that the United States suffers from a "saving shortfall," see Blecker (1990a, 1990b, 1991a), Block (1990), Lipsey and Kravis (1987), Eisner (1991), and Steindl (1990). For present purposes, however, I take the official national income account data which show a declining U.S. private saving rate at their face value.

7   This reduction in Japanese investment was largely a fall in housing investment, not business investment, and thus did not have any negative repercussions for Japanese competitiveness. For further discussion of this issue see Chapter 5.

8   Similar calculations are made by Lawrence (1990, pp. 367–68).

9   The fact that this last index was still 10 percent above its 1980 level in 1990 is accounted for by the fact that it includes many developing country currencies, while the other indexes only include industrial country currencies. Most developing countries have managed exchange rates, and did not experience real appreciations in the 1980s as the European nations and Japan did. One weakness of the Dallas Fed index (as well as the Federal Reserve Board G-10 index) is that it uses

consumer price indexes to measure price levels, rather than indexes of tradeable goods.

10 All trade data in this paragraph are derived from the national income and product accounts. The current account is measured by "net foreign investment" in the national income accounts; this variable is not available in constant dollars.

11 See Friedman (1988) for an analysis of U.S. monetary policy in the 1980s; see Greider (1987) on the politics of monetary policy.

12 Some economists claim that it was the expectation of future budget deficits which drove the dollar up in 1981. See, for example, Feldstein (1986) and Branson (1985). However, the tight monetary policy and high interest rates in effect at that time (1981) seem to offer a more parsimonious (and believable) explanation of the initial run-up in the dollar, as pointed out by Frenkel (1985) among others.

13 The nominal money supply (M1) grew by 5.7 percent from December 1983 to December 1984, the lowest annual rate since the 4.8 percent from December 1974 to December 1975—a recession period. A broader measure, M2, grew somewhat faster in 1984—8.3 percent—but this was still the lowest rate of M2 growth since 1979. Another indicator of monetary tightness is the percentage of the increase in the net federal debt to the public which was purchased by the Federal Reserve Banks, which fell from 11.1 percent in 1981 to 4.5 percent in 1984. This shows a diminishing willingness of the Fed to monetize the growing federal government deficits.

14 The money supply (M1) grew by 12.4 percent in 1985 and 17.0 percent in 1986, far exceeding even the growth rates experienced in the inflationary years of the 1970s. Contrary to monetarist doctrine, this monetary growth did not rekindle rapid inflation in the late 1980s. Another indicator of monetary loosening is the fact that the percentage of the net increase in federal debt purchased by the Fed rose to 14.0 percent in 1986 (compare previous endnote).

15 Helkie and Hooper (1988, Table 2–17, p. 48) report that the real (CPI-adjusted) value of the dollar against the G-10 currencies plus 8 LDC currencies, using multilateral weights, rose by 48 percent from 1980 to 1985. Their model simulations indicate that a 3.5 percent of GNP fiscal expansion in the United States would have appreciated the dollar by only 10.5 percent in real terms over that same period. According to comparisons made in Bryant et al. (1988, Table 4–6, p. 74), the model used by Helkie and Hooper (the Multicountry Model [MCM] of the Federal Reserve Board) is not unusually low in its estimates of the effects of fiscal stimulus on the value of the dollar. For a 1 percent of GNP fiscal expansion, the MCM model predicts a 3.9 percent increase in the value of the dollar after 6 years, compared with a high of 7.0 percent (Japanese Economic Planning Agency model) and a low of −9.9 percent (Wharton Econometrics model). In the short run, the MCM model predicts the biggest positive effect of fiscal expansion on the dollar (a 1.7 percent appreciation after 1 year).

[16] The figures cited in this paragraph are derived from data in Helkie and Hooper (1988), Table 2–12, p. 41. Agricultural exports and oil imports are excluded from these figures because Helkie and Hooper do not report the relative price effects separately for those commodities. Since including those commodities adds only $1 billion to the total merchandise deficit, the main conclusions stated here are not affected by excluding them.

[17] Relative supplies are measured by the ratio of U.S. to foreign capital stocks. Since this ratio tends to fall over time, the effects which Helkie and Hooper attribute to relative supply shifts may be taken as a proxy for the effects of declining compet itiveness, as argued by Krugman and Baldwin (1987). This point is discussed further in Chapter 3.

[18] The Helkie-Hooper estimate of the effect of U.S. fiscal expansion is actually based on a rather crude extrapolation of the simulation results for the MCM model reported in the Bryant et al. comparison of models. Those results show a sustained 1 percent of GNP fiscal expansion in the U.S. causing the U.S. current account to fall by about $10 billion after 1 year, $17 billion after 2 years, $23 billion after 3 years, and $53 billion after 6 years. Helkie and Hooper state that, based on these results, they "have chosen to estimate" the current account effect of U.S. fiscal expansion as a fall of $20 billion for each 1 percent of GNP of fiscal stimulus—apparently, the effect after 2½ years (since 20 is half way between 17 and 23). Then they multiplied this figure by 3.5 (the approximate percentage of GNP by which the U.S. fiscal deficit rose in 1980–85) to obtain the estimate of a $70 billion fall in the current account. It should be noted that this procedure exaggerates the effects of the actual shift in U.S. fiscal policy, since some part of the 3.5 percent of GNP increase in the actual U.S. federal deficit must be attributed to the foreign demand contraction combined with U.S. competitive decline.

[19] Most of the remainder of this increase is attributed to the "additional" dollar appreciation in 1980–85—i.e., the part of the dollar's rise which is not explained by fiscal policies (and is presumably due to monetary contraction plus the speculative bubble).

[20] See Eisner (1989) for an analysis of the positive effects of budget deficits.

[21] The following analysis draws upon Blecker (1991b).

Chapter 3

Evidence for a Secular Decline in Competitiveness

In order to explain the depth and persistence of U.S. trade problems, it is clearly necessary to go beyond an exclusive focus on macro policies. By its nature, a structural deterioration in competitiveness adds to the trade deficit slowly over time. This is exactly why the macro policy effects seem so dominant for the 1980–87 period. But the policy-induced worsening of the U.S. trade position in the 1980s was superimposed upon a pre-existing, underlying trend of declining U.S. competitiveness. Over a longer period of time, the continual erosion of competitive advantages shifts the very terrain on which macro policies operate, implying a greater trade deficit for any given set of macro policies and exchange rates.

This chapter will show that there is clear and compelling evidence for a declining trend in the U.S. trade position. Three types of evidence will be discussed. First, the real value (purchasing power) of the dollar which would enable the United States to balance its trade has decreased steadily over time. Second, the response of U.S. exports to foreign income growth is much smaller than the response of U.S. imports to domestic income growth. This implies that, for any given value of the dollar, the U.S. economy is constrained to grow more slowly than the rest of the world in order to maintain balanced trade; more rapid growth in the U.S. can only come at the expense of widening trade deficits and increasing indebtedness to foreign countries. And third, U.S. nonoil imports have grown by roughly $98 billion more in the past ten years (measured in constant 1982

The continual erosion of competitive advantages shifts the very terrain on which macro policies operate.

dollars) than can be accounted for by changes in import prices, exchange rates, and national income—the variables that reflect macroeconomic policies. We now turn to examine each of these three types of evidence.

The Falling Trend of the Dollar

Looking at the historical record of the last two decades, it is clear that the dollar had to depreciate in real terms (i.e., more than enough to compensate for U.S. inflation relative to foreign inflation) in order to prevent growing trade deficits—and that those deficits have grown when the dollar did not depreciate. This point can be seen clearly by comparing the behavior of the trade balance and the dollar since the Bretton Woods system of fixed exchange rates was abandoned in the early 1970s.

Figure 6 shows the merchandise trade balance and the current account balance, both measured as percentages of GNP.[1] Note that the current account remained balanced on average in the 1970s, in spite of some fluctuations. The merchandise balance had a downward trend, but this was mainly due to the rising price of oil imports. The current

Figure 6
Alternative Measures of the U.S. Trade Balance
as a Percent of GNP, Quarterly 1970-1990

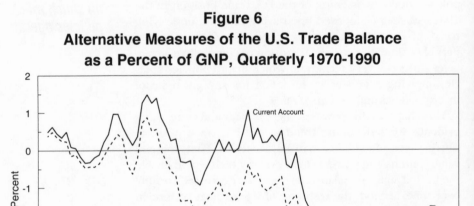

Source: Department of Commerce, BEA.
Note: Current account balance is measured by net foreign investment. Data for 1990:4 are preliminary.

account balance was higher than the merchandise balance mainly because of net investment income from abroad. In the 1980s, however, both balances turned sharply negative together, and the gap between them shrank as net investment income from abroad dried up (due to increasing U.S. foreign debt). By both measures, the trade deficit peaked in 1987 and fell thereafter. But as of 1990, the trade deficit still remained at about 2 percent of GNP by either measure (merchandise or current account balance).

Figure 7 shows that the real merchandise trade balance in constant 1982 dollars was negative on average, but with no declining trend, from 1970 to 1980.[2] The real merchandise trade balance then fell sharply from 1980 to 1986. The real balance began to improve in 1987 while the nominal balance continued to deteriorate, as the falling dollar raised current import prices (the J-Curve effect). After four years of improvement, the real trade deficit still averaged over $100 for the year 1990 (it improved notably in the fourth quarter, but mainly as a result of the recession which cut U.S. import demand).

After four years of improvement, the real trade deficit still averaged over $100 for the year 1990.

Figure 7
Real U.S. Merchandise Trade Balance,
Quarterly 1970-1990

Source: Department of Commerce, BEA.
Note: Data for 1990:4 are preliminary.

59

Figure 8 shows two indices of the real value of the dollar. One index, compiled by the Federal Reserve Board of Governors, measures the trade-weighted value of the dollar against the ten leading industrial country currencies, corrected for consumer price inflation. This will be called the G-10 index. A broader index, compiled by the Federal Reserve Bank of Dallas, includes many more countries—a total of 101, including the NICs and most developing countries. This is called the RX-101 index. While it is possible to construct many other indices, using different groups of countries, different weighting schemes, and different inflation measures (see Pauls, 1987), these two indices—one relatively narrow, the other much broader—will suffice for present purposes.

Both indices in Figure 8 reveal a downward trend in the value of the dollar in the 1970s.

Both indices in Figure 8 reveal a downward trend in the value of the dollar in the 1970s, followed by a sharp increase in 1981–85, and an even sharper decline in 1985–88. According to the G-10 measure, the dollar recovered slightly in 1989 before dropping to about its 1980 real value in 1990. However, the dollar remained about 10 percent above its 1980 real value in 1990 according to the

Figure 8
Alternative Measures of the Real Value of the
U.S. Dollar, Quarterly 1971-1990

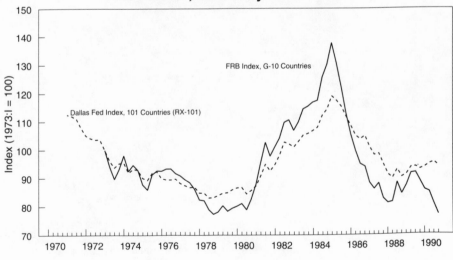

Sources: Federal Reserve Board of Governors and Federal Reserve Bank of Dallas.

RX-101 measure, due to the inclusion of developing country and NIC currencies (see also Table 2). Throughout this period, the broader RX-101 index fluctuated less widely than the narrower G-10 measure.

Comparing Figure 8 with Figure 6, we see that the dollar was more or less continuously falling while the current account remained essentially balanced (or in surplus) throughout the 1970s. To be sure, there were current account deficits in 1971 and again in 1977–78, but they were relatively small and more than offset by surpluses in the rest of the decade—thanks to the continued depreciation of the dollar. Comparing Figure 8 with Figure 7, we can see that the real merchandise trade balance (in constant 1982 dollars) was in a deficit throughout the 1970s, but with no declining trend, while the dollar was falling in real terms. *The fact that a continuous real depreciation of the dollar was necessary to maintain current account balance and to keep the merchandise trade deficit from worsening indicates an underlying declining trend of U.S. competitiveness in the 1970s.*

The problem in the early 1980s was not simply that the dollar rose, but more precisely that *it rose when it needed to fall further.* To make this point, Figure 9 extrapolates the 1971–1980 trend of the RX-101 index[3] into the 1981–1990 period. The trend is plotted on a logarithmic scale, which represents a trend with a constant proportional rate of change as a straight line. Along this trend line, the dollar fell at an average rate of 2.7 percent per year from 1971 to 1980. Extending this trend line to 1990 gives a rough indication of the exchange rate adjustment which would have been required to maintain current account balance in the 1980s.

Viewed against this benchmark, the rise in the dollar in the mid-1980s is truly astounding. From 1980–85, the dollar moved in the *opposite* direction from that which would have been necessary to offset declining competitiveness. Moreover, this way of viewing the problem shows that relying on dollar depreciation to solve the trade deficit is like shooting at a moving target. Although the dollar fell to just above its 1980 level in 1990, it was still far above the extrapolated 1970s trend line. The fact that a merchandise trade deficit of over $100 billion and a current account deficit of $86 billion persisted in 1990, in spite of the fact that the dollar had returned to nearly its 1980 real value, is dramatic evidence that the dollar would have to fall much fur-

From 1980–85, the dollar moved in the opposite direction from that which would have been necessary to offset declining competitiveness.

Figure 9
Real Value of Dollar Against 101 Currencies,
Actual 1971-1990 vs. Trend for 1971-1980

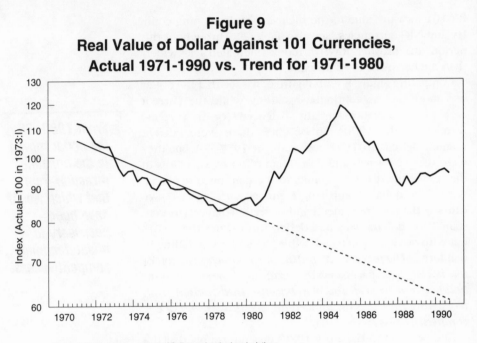

Sources: Federal Reserve Bank of Dallas and author's calculations.
Note: Data plotted on logarithmic scale, using quarterly data.

*If the real
exchange rate
does not adjust,
then U.S. national
income is
constrained to
grow more slowly
than the income
of the rest of the
world.*

ther in order to achieve balanced trade through exchange rate adjustment.

Unequal Income Elasticities

Another way of conceptualizing the secular decline in the U.S. trade position originated in the work of Houthakker and Magee (1969). They found that the income elasticity of U.S. demand for imports was significantly higher than the income elasticity of foreign demand for U.S. exports.[4] These unequal elasticities imply that, for U.S. and foreign income to grow at equal rates over time, the real value of the dollar (the relative price of American goods) would have to fall in the long run in order to prevent secularly rising U.S. trade deficits. Alternatively, if the real exchange rate does not adjust, then U.S. national income is constrained to grow more slowly than the income of the rest of the world (see the discussion of "income adjustment" in Chapter 1, above). A. P. Thirlwall (1979) has called this phenomenon "balance-of-payments-constrained growth."

62

Table 4 shows Houthakker and Magee's original estimates of the income elasticities of U.S. import and export demand along with some more recent estimates, including new ones made for this study. Two recent articles seem to show that the gap between these elasticities might be small or nonexistent. Krugman and Baldwin's (1987) estimated income elasticities are both at the high end of the spectrum, with only a slightly higher elasticity for imports. Helkie and Hooper's (1988) estimated income elasticities are virtually the same for exports and imports (2.19 versus 2.11).

However, the secular decline in U.S. competitiveness shows up in Helkie and Hooper's model in a different way. They argue that traditional measures of income elasticities of import and export demand may actually capture the effects of changing supply conditions. In order to identify the true demand responses, they add a variable to control for supply conditions: "the ratio of home to foreign productive capital stocks" (pp. 20–21). Since the ratio of the U.S. to rest-of-world capital stocks has fallen throughout most of the sample period, this variable essentially picks up the negative secular trend in the U.S. trade balance.[5] As noted earlier, Helkie and Hooper find that this variable accounted for a $26 billion rise in the (nonoil, nonagricultural) merchandise trade deficit from 1980 to 1986, or about one-sixth of the total rise between those years. From a policy perspective, however, it makes little difference whether the need for the dollar to fall (or for U.S. income to grow more slowly) is attributed to changes in "supply" as opposed to "demand" conditions.

The estimates by Cline (1989) and Lawrence (1990) support the traditional (Houthakker-Magee) view that the income elasticity for U.S. imports is considerably higher than for U.S. exports. Cline's estimates are especially noteworthy because they are derived from a disaggregated model of U.S. trade with 16 other countries and country groups, rather than aggregate export and import demand functions. Cline finds that the weighted average income elasticities for U.S. trade with all 16 other countries are 1.70 for exports and 2.44 for imports. Based on Thirlwall's (1979) model, as interpreted more recently by Davidson (1990–91), this difference implies that U.S. income would have to grow about two-thirds as fast as foreign income in order to prevent growing trade deficits, if the dollar

The secular decline in U.S. competitiveness shows up in Helkie and Hooper's model in a different way.

63

TABLE 4
Estimated Income-Elasticities of U.S. Export and Import Demand

Author(s)	Sample Period	Other Variables Included	Income Elasticity Exports	Imports
Houthakker and Magee (1969)	1951–1966 (annual)	Relative prices	0.99	1.51
Krugman and Baldwin (1987)[a]	1977:2–86:4 (quarterly)	Relative prices	2.42	2.87
Helkie and Hooper (1988)[b]	1969:1–84:4 (quarterly)	Relative prices Relative supplies Dock strikes Capacity utilization (imports only)	2.19	2.11
Cline (1989)[c]	1973:1–87:4 (quarterly)	Relative prices Cross-prices	1.70	2.44
Lawrence (1990)[d]	1976:1–90:1 (quarterly)	Relative Prices	1.60	2.47
This Report[e]	1975:1–89:4 (quarterly)	Relative Prices	1.50	2.56

Sources: Houthakker and Magee (1969), Table 1, p. 113; Cline (1989), Table 4.3, p. 155; Helkie and Hooper (1988), Table 2–4, p. 21; Krugman and Baldwin (1987), Tables 1 and 2, pp. 17–18; Lawrence (1990), Tables 8 and 10, pp. 360, 365.

Notes:
[a]Estimates are for U.S. nonagricultural exports and nonoil imports. Relative prices are measured by a real exchange rate index for 6 industrialized countries and 2 NICs. The income measure is domestic expenditures.
[b]Estimates are for U.S. nonagricultural exports and nonoil imports (with gold and silver also excluded). The income measure is GNP. Relative prices are measured by implicit deflators for nonagricultural exports and nonpetroleum imports. Relative supplies are proxied by relative capital stocks.
[c]Trade-weighted averages of estimated bilateral elasticities with 16 other countries; some of the individual bilateral elasticities were constrained to upper limits. Cross-prices were included to capture international competition in third markets.
[d]Estimates are for nonoil, noncomputer imports and nonagricultural, noncomputer exports. Relative prices are measured by the author's price indexes which exclude computers. The income-elasticity for imports is the sum of the elasticities for potential GDP and actual domestic demand. The foreign income variable is domestic demand in other OECD countries weighted by 1980 U.S. export shares.
[e]Estimates are for U.S. nonagricultural exports and nonpetroleum imports. The export elasticity is taken from equation (5.5) in Appendix Table A-5, using rest-of-world GDP as the income variable. The import elasticity is from equation (1.11) in Appendix Table A-1, using U.S. domestic expenditures as the income variable. See endnote 43 and the Appendix for more details.

remains constant in real terms (since 1.70 is about two-thirds of 2.44).

Some new estimates of the income elasticities, based on the econometric analysis in the Appendix of this report, are given in the last row of Table 4. My best estimates are that these elasticities are 1.50 for exports and 2.56 for imports. These estimates were chosen from the range of estimates in the Appendix based on a combination of statistical criteria and a desire to give a conservative portrayal of the gap.[6] These figures are close to those of Cline and Lawrence, and support the traditional Houthakker-Magee view. According to these estimates, U.S. income can only grow about 60 percent as fast as foreign income in order to prevent growing trade deficits, for any given real value of the dollar. This is further support for the hypothesis of a declining trend of American competitiveness.

U.S. income can only grow about 60 percent as fast as foreign income in order to prevent growing trade deficits, for any given real value of the dollar.

The Cumulative Impact of Declining Competitiveness

An alternative methodology for estimating the secular trend in competitiveness is found in Krugman and Baldwin (1987). This method is to estimate a time trend in the import and export demand equations, after controlling for the other factors (mainly relative price and income variables) which affect demand, including any lagged effects. The logic behind this method is that all macroeconomic policies—whether fiscal or monetary, domestic or foreign—affect import and export demand through their effects on relative prices of domestic and foreign products (including exchange rate effects) and relative national incomes (domestic versus foreign). Thus, whatever part of the import or export demand is *not* explained by these variables can be attributed to other, "structural" factors. If these factors operate more or less continually over time, they should be captured by a time trend.

Krugman and Baldwin found that the time trend was negative and significant for exports, but also negative (although statistically insignificant)[7] for imports, based on estimates for the period 1977:1 to 1986:4 (see their Table 3, p. 19). They argued that the negative time trend for exports was exaggerated, however, because when the time trend is included in their export demand equation, the income elasticity rises to an implausible magnitude (5.54, compared with 2.42 without a time trend). Thus Krugman and Baldwin's results were inconclusive.

My estimates of import and export demand equations are presented in the Appendix. As explained in more detail there, I essentially follow Krugman and Baldwin's method, but I use more recent data (up to 1989:4) and try a variety of alternative specifications designed to test the sensitivity of the results to particular choices of how to measure the variables, what time period to include, etc. I also use a statistical technique called "differencing" to try to obtain more reliable estimates of the time trend. I find that the evidence for a structural decline in export performance is still inconclusive. However, I find robust evidence for a structural rising tendency of (nonoil) imports, above and beyond what can be explained by the changing relative price of imports and the growth of U.S. national income (or domestic expenditures) in the 1980s.

The rising trend of import demand due to structural factors is estimated to be about 3.1 percent per year in the 1980s.

The rising trend of import demand due to structural factors is estimated to be about 3.1 percent per year in the 1980s. As explained in the Appendix, this is a mid-range estimate which is based on the most statistically reliable specification of the import demand equation. Cumulated over the decade 1980–89, this would imply a structural increase in nonoil merchandise imports of $106.6 billion in constant 1982 dollars. This cumulative impact is of the same magnitude as the merchandise trade deficit for the year 1989, which was $108.5 billion in constant 1982 dollars.[8] If this trend continues, it would imply further increases in import demand of $12.6 billion in 1990 and $13.1 billion in 1991 (in 1982 dollars), holding all other factors (including oil prices and the recession) constant.

Like any econometric estimate, the $106.6 billion figure must be used with caution. There are some factors that could cause a spurious impression of a significant time trend in the equation for import demand. One of these factors would be mismeasurement of the quantity of "real" imports, if the mismeasurement were biased upward over time. In fact, such a problem may exist in the National Income and Product Accounts (NIPAs) measure of the "real" quantity of nonpetroleum imports in 1982 dollars. The NIPAs value computers at the 1982 prices of their "hedonic" attributes (e.g., memory capacity, processing speed). Since the prices of these attributes fell sharply after 1982, real quantities of computer imports are exaggerated for the late 1980s by being valued at 1982 prices (see Denison, 1989; U.S. Congressional Budget Office, 1990; Lawrence, 1990; Meade, 1990). This undoubtedly imparts

66

some upward bias to the NIPA measure of constant dollar nonpetroleum imports for the 1980s.[9]

However, this upward bias is not large enough to eliminate most of the rising secular trend in imports. I estimate that imports of computers and information processing equipment in 1989 were about $67 billion in 1982 dollars, or 17 percent of nonpetroleum imports; the corresponding figures in current dollars were $36 billion and 8 percent.[10] This suggests that the "real" volume of computer imports should perhaps be cut in half to obtain a less biased estimate. That would lower total 1989 nonpetroleum imports (in 1982 dollars) from $405.5 billion to $372 billion, a reduction of about 8 percent. If we then take 8 percent off our estimated cumulative structural increase in imports, we would still have an increase of about $98 billion for the decade 1980–89.[11]

It is important to be precise about the meaning of this estimated structural rise in imports. In economic terms, it is the amount by which the *import demand function* shifted out during the 1980s. That is, for any given relative price of imports and level of domestic expenditures, imports would have been about $98 billion higher in 1989 than they were in 1979. This does not mean that the merchandise trade *deficit* would have been exactly $98 billion lower, however. Since higher imports reduce national income (all else being equal), a structural tendency for imports to increase implies a structural tendency for national income to be reduced (relative to its trend), and this would partly offset the rise in the trade deficit. Since imports are roughly 12 percent of U.S. GNP (in constant 1982 dollars), the cumulative decline in the trade balance over 1980–89 would be about $86 billion, or nearly 80 percent of the actual deficit in 1989. Table 5 summarizes the various adjustments which were made to obtain this $86 billion figure for the structural deterioration in the trade balance.

This estimated structural component of the trade deficit is consistent with the estimate obtained recently by Lawrence (1990), using a different method. Lawrence argues that (after correcting for the problems in measuring computer prices), relative import and export prices at the end of the 1980s were back to about their 1980 levels, while U.S. and foreign income growth rates over the whole decade were very similar (see the data in Table 2, above, for confirmation). Nevertheless, the merchandise trade bal-

The cumulative decline in the trade balance over 1980–89 would be about $86 billion, or nearly 80 percent of the actual deficit in 1989.

TABLE 5
Estimated Cumulative Impact of Structural Trend Decline in Competitiveness on Imports and the Trade Balance, 1980–89, in billions of 1982 dollars

Cumulative increase in nonpetroleum imports	$ 106.6
Less part attributed to overvaluation of computers	− 8.6
Corrected increase in nonpetroleum imports	98.0
Less induced reduction in import demand due to lower national income	− 12.0
Cumulative structural increase in trade deficit	86.0

Note: See text for explanation.

ance (excluding oil imports, agricultural exports, *and* computer trade) was $75.2 billion lower at the end of the decade. Including computers, the corresponding figure is an $86.2 billion decline (in 1982 dollars)—or $80.7 billion, if we cut the increase in the computer deficit in half due to the measurement problem. Thus our estimate of the structural decline in the U.S. trade position is roughly consistent with other studies, and may be regarded as a reasonable order of magnitude.

Endnotes

1   These series are taken from the national income and product accounts (NIPAs), and thus differ slightly from the international transactions (balance of payments) series. The current account is measured by "net foreign investment."

2   There is no comparable constant dollar series for the current account. The NIPA measure of "net exports of goods and services" is available in constant dollars, but this measure excludes government interest payments to foreigners which rose sharply in the 1980s, as well as unilateral transfers.

3   The RX-101 index is used since it shows more moderate fluctuations. However, using the G-10 index would yield similar conclusions.

4   The income elasticity is defined as the percentage by which demand (for imports or exports) rises when income (domestic or foreign, respectively) rises by 1 percent.

5   This point is recognized by Krugman and Baldwin (1987, pp. 35–36): "the downward trend was reintroduced [in Helkie and Hooper's model] by the fact that capacity [capital stock] grew more rapidly in the rest of the world than in the United States."

6   Both estimates were taken from equations without time trends and with the data measured in levels of natural logarithms for comparability with other studies. Both were estimated using data for 1975–1989, the longest time period for which all relevant data series were available. The elasticity for imports is taken from equation (1.11) in Table A-1 in the Appendix. This equation uses a direct measure of import prices, rather than an exchange rate index, and measures income by domestic expenditures rather than GNP. The elasticity for exports is taken from equation (5.5) in Table A-5 in the Appendix. This equation uses the G-10 dollar index to convert U.S. export prices into foreign prices, and measures foreign income by non-U.S. OECD gross domestic product. This specification yields the best statistical fit (highest R^2) of the export regressions run over 1975–1989 in log levels. The estimate of 1.50 for the export elasticity is near the high end of my estimates of this parameter, while the estimate of 2.56 for the import elasticity is near the low end of my estimates of the latter. Thus the choice of these estimates is, if anything, biased against finding a large gap.

7   An estimate is said to be statistically insignificant if it is small relative to the error in its measurement.

8   Calculated from the National Income and Product Accounts, in *Survey of Current Business,* July 1990, Table 4.2.

9   For further discussion of this issue see the Appendix.

10 These estimates were made by taking the percentage of information processing and related equipment in total nonresidential producers' durable equipment

investment (from Tables 5.12 and 5.13 of the NIPAs), and applying these percentages to imports of capital goods except autos (from Tables 4.3 and 4.4). Consumer demand for computers for personal use is relatively small and may be ignored.

[11] Reducing the growth rate of the trend increase in imports by 8 percent, from about 3.1 to 2.8 percent per year, results in a similar cumulative total of $99 billion. The figure reported in the text, which is simply 92 percent of $106.6 billion, is thus a more conservative estimate.

Chapter 4

Structural Roots of U.S. Trade Problems: An Overview

Competitiveness is inherently a relative concept. If U.S. industrial competitiveness has declined, this decline must be matched by an improvement in the competitiveness of its major trading partners. The first part of this chapter seeks to identify those countries whose trade performance has improved, relative to that of the United States, in the past decade. Three main groups of countries stand out in this analysis: the technologically advanced industrial surplus countries (mainly Japan and Germany), the supercompetitive East Asian NICs (especially South Korea and Taiwan), and the Latin American debtors. The diverse nature of those countries suggests further that American competitive decline is multifaceted, and that the causes of this decline may differ in regard to different trading partners. The last part of this chapter then outlines some hypotheses concerning this variegated pattern of competitive realignment.

American competitive decline is multifaceted, and . . . the causes of this decline may differ in regard to different trading partners.

Changes in Trade Performance

One common indicator of competitiveness is market shares. Figure 10 shows the changing shares of the G-7 industrial countries in total OECD[1] exports of manufactures to the world from 1980 to 1985 and 1988. The shares of the U.S., the U.K., and France generally fell, while the shares of Japan and Canada generally rose, and the shares of Germany and Italy showed no upward or downward trend. Although these shares are affected by changing exchange rates (since all other countries' trade is converted to U.S.

dollars), the data in Figure 10 do provide evidence for a declining U.S. relative position in terms of where the world spends its money for manufactured goods.

Another indicator of trade performance is changes in bilateral trade balances. Table 6 compares U.S. merchandise trade balances with the nation's leading trading partners in 1979 and 1988. These are good years to compare since they were both late-expansion years in the U.S. business cycle. While the trade balance deteriorated with almost every major country or region (with the sole exceptions of the Middle East and Africa)[2] over this period, the three blocs of nations mentioned above account for almost the entire decline. When just three countries (Japan, West Germany, and Canada) are omitted, the U.S. still has a surplus (albeit a diminished one) with the other industrialized (OECD) countries in 1988. The increase in the bilateral deficit with Japan alone accounts for 45 percent of the increase in the overall deficit; Japan and West Germany together account for more than half of the increase. The four leading East Asian NICs (Taiwan, South Korea, Singapore, and Hong Kong) account for another quarter of the

The increase in the bilateral deficit with Japan alone accounts for 45 percent of the increase in the overall deficit.

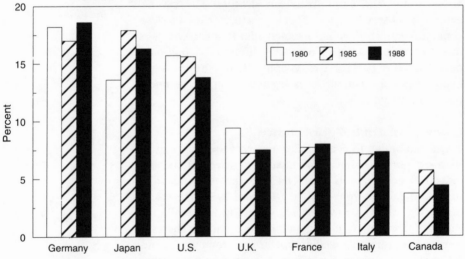

Figure 10
G-7 Country Shares of Total OECD Manufactured Exports to World in 1980, 1985, and 1988

Sources: OECD, Foreign Trade by Commodities, various issues and OECD Microtables 1979-80 Data.
Note: Manufactured exports are sum of SITC's 5+6+7+8.

increase in the deficit. And U.S. trade with Latin America went from a surplus to a deficit, with the net decline accounting for about 10 percent of the overall decline.

Simply comparing the changes in bilateral trade balances shown in Table 6 is not sufficient, however. An apparently large bilateral deficit could just be a reflection of a large volume of bilateral trade. In order to correct for this problem, Table 7 provides a measure of how large each bilateral deficit is in proportion to the total volume of bilateral trade. The "trade imbalance index" is defined as the ratio of the trade balance (exports minus imports) to the total value of trade (exports plus imports) with each country or region.

Comparing Tables 6 and 7, we see that while the 1988 U.S. deficit with Canada is large in dollar terms, the imbalance index with Canada is less (in absolute value) than the average for all countries in that year, and had increased very little since 1979. Thus the large deficit with Canada is mainly a function of the fact that Canada is the United States' largest trading partner. In contrast, the Japanese and West German imbalance indexes are far above the average (in absolute value), indicating that these imbalances are out of proportion to the extent of U.S. trade with them. The other countries with significantly higher-than-average imbalance indexes in 1988 are the Asian nations, both the "Four Tigers" (Korea, Taiwan, Hong Kong, and Singapore) and the other Asian countries (especially China, Thailand, India, and Malaysia).

The last column of Table 7 shows the *changes* in the imbalance indexes between 1979 and 1988. Above average increases are found in the cases of Japan, West Germany, the "Four Tigers," and other Asian countries. In addition, some countries which had relatively low negative (or even positive) imbalance indexes for 1988 nevertheless had relatively large negative changes between 1979 and 1988. This group includes other OECD countries, Latin America, Eastern Europe, and the Soviet Union.

Of course, one would not expect the "imbalance indexes" to be the same for all countries. Even if overall U.S. trade were balanced, there would still be bilateral deficits with some countries and surpluses with others. Nevertheless, the worsening bilateral imbalances are so concentrated with certain countries and regions that it is necessary to pay attention to their particular economic structures and macro policies when explaining how

The worsening bilateral imbalances are so concentrated with certain countries and regions that it is necessary to pay attention to their particular economic structures and macro policies.

TABLE 6
U.S. Merchandise Trade Balance
By Major Country Groups, 1979 and 1988
(in billions of U.S. dollars)

Country or Region	1979	1988	Change
Japan	-8.8	-52.1	-43.3
West Germany	-2.7	-12.2	-9.5
Canada	-4.9	-11.7	-6.8
Other OECD	15.6	3.0	-12.6
"Four Tigers"[a]	-3.6	-28.4	-25.0
Other Asian	-1.8	-9.9	-8.1
Latin America	1.4	-8.8	-10.2
Middle East[b]	-4.0	-0.7	+3.3
Africa	-18.2	-3.4	+14.8
Eastern Europe & U.S.S.R.	3.8	1.5	-2.3
World Total[c]	-25.3	-120.9	-95.6

Sources: OECD, *Monthly Statistics of Foreign Trade,* April 1989, and *Statistics of Foreign Trade: Monthly Bulletin,* February 1982, and author's calculations.

Notes:
[a]South Korea, Taiwan, Hong Kong, and Singapore.
[b]Excludes North African countries (which are included with Africa) and Turkey (which is included in other OECD).
[c]Includes some countries not listed separately.

changes in competitive capabilities have influenced the overall U.S. trade deficit.

This focus on bilateral relationships may seem to be at odds with the conventional emphasis on the macroeconomic character of the trade balance. For example, the 1987 *Economic Report of the President* stated that:

The deterioration of the U.S. trade balance is too pervasive to be credibly explained by analyses focused on a product-by-product, country-by-country basis. Rather, the great bulk of the widespread deterioration must be viewed as a product of general macroeconomic developments in the United States and the rest of the world. (U.S. Council of Economic Advisors, 1987, p. 99)

TABLE 7
Trade Imbalance Index[a]
By Major Country Groups, 1979 and 1988

Country or Region	1979	1988	Change
Japan	−0.201	−0.408	−0.207
West Germany	−0.137	−0.298	−0.161
Canada	−0.069	−0.078	−0.009
Other OECD	0.189	0.019	−0.170
"Four Tigers"[b]	−0.131	−0.289	−0.158
Other Asian	−0.099	−0.235	−0.136
Latin America	0.028	−0.099	−0.127
Middle East[c]	−0.152	−0.029	+0.123
Africa	−0.595	−0.188	+0.407
Eastern Europe & U.S.S.R.	0.505	0.257	−0.248
World Average[d]	−0.065	−0.159 −	0.094

Sources: OECD, *Monthly Statistics of Foreign Trade.* April 1989, and *Statistics of Foreign Trade: Monthly Bulletin,* February 1982, and author's calculations.

Notes:
[a]Computed as the ratio of (exports-imports)/(exports + imports).
[b]South Korea, Taiwan, Hong Kong, and Singapore.
[c]Excludes North African countries (which are included with Africa) and Turkey (which is included in other OECD).
[d]Includes some countries not listed separately.

But this argument is based on a false opposition between aggregative relationships and their individual components.[3] The "rest of the world" is not some kind of ethereal entity hovering above the globe, but a set of actual nations with which the United States trades. The largest of these nations (in terms of their trade with the U.S.) must be counted as significant components of the macroeconomic aggregates.

The traditional argument for ignoring bilateral analysis is in fact just a special case of the traditional argument against considering competitiveness factors in analyzing the trade balance. The argument is that a worsening in the bilateral balance with any one country, no matter how large, would inevitably be offset by an improvement with the rest of the world. Ultimately, this boils down to another version of the same old story about exchange rates. If, say, the U.S. deficit rises with Japan, the dollar should fall enough against other countries' currencies for the U.S. to run a surplus with all other countries large enough to offset the deficit with Japan. But if, as argued in Chapter 1, this automatic adjustment process does not necessarily work, then increased bilateral deficits with some countries are not automatically offset by bilateral surpluses with others.

A Conceptual Framework

The changing position of the United States in the world economy can be analyzed in terms of the "product cycle" model of international trade, originally due to Vernon (1966). In the immediate postwar period (roughly 1945–1965), the United States stood more or less alone as the dominant technological leader in the Western world. Most innovations tended to occur here,[4] and (aside from agricultural commodities) the U.S. specialized in exports of new or innovative manufactured products—especially goods embodying labor-saving technology. As new products "matured," their production was transferred initially to other industrialized countries (Western Europe and Japan), while the U.S. continued to develop still newer products. When goods became fully standardized, their production could then be shifted to the low-wage underdeveloped countries. Thus, the U.S. trade pattern (in manufactures) has been to export "technology-intensive" products and to import standardized products. Or, as Dosi, Pavitt, and Soete (1990) put it, trade in innovative products is determined by absolute technological advantages, while trade in standardized manufactures is determined by comparative labor costs.

As this pattern of trade has evolved over the last 25 years, however, problems have arisen for the U.S. on two sides. On one side, there has been a notable convergence of other industrialized countries, especially Japan and West Germany, toward the United States in technological leadership. Both Japan and Germany have been catching up rapidly in productivity levels, and both have become major centers of technological innovation (see Soete, 1985; Baumol, Blackman, and Wolff, 1989). On the other side, the last two decades have witnessed a phenomenal industrialization of some formerly underdeveloped countries, both in East Asia and (in spite of the debt crisis) in Latin America as well. An

76

important component of this process has been the acceleration of technology transfers from the U.S. and other industrialized countries to the NICs.

To some extent, the convergence process with other industrial countries is inevitable and benign; they would naturally tend to catch up technologically in a period of generally open markets and peaceful commerce. However, to the extent that the loss of U.S. technological leadership is due to activist industrial policies abroad which have had no counterpart at home, the U.S. may fall further behind in the innovation race than is necessary, with potentially serious consequences for domestic living standards. This seems to have been particularly true in the case of Japan (see Salvatore, 1990). In any case, the historical analogies given by the proponents of the "convergence" hypothesis (e.g., England in the 19th century) are not necessarily reassuring. In past cases, the rising industrial powers (e.g., the United States and Germany before World War I) did not merely catch up to the former leader, but rather surpassed it.

American industrial growth and comparative advantages in trade in the period 1880–1940 were based on the intensive exploitation of the country's natural resources.

The importance of maintaining leadership in technological innovation follows from the *cumulative* nature of the innovation process: new innovations tend to build on past progress, even at the level of the individual firm (Rosenberg, 1976 and 1982; Freeman, 1982). If U.S. producers cease to participate in this cumulative process in one field after another, it may become harder and harder for them to keep up. The ever-growing international mobility of knowledge as well as capital can mitigate this problem to some extent, as argued by Mowery and Rosenberg (1989). That is, U.S. producers can now benefit from reverse technology transfers from Japan or elsewhere. But this does not necessarily mean that U.S.-based producers can get back on the innovative fast track without the help of government policies—especially when competing with foreign producers aided by their own governments (e.g., the European airplane consortium or the Japanese supercomputer effort).

A special factor influencing both overall U.S. industrial performance and the U.S. trade balance is the role of energy and natural resources. As Wright (1990) demonstrated, American industrial growth and comparative advantages in trade in the period 1880–1940 were based on the intensive exploitation of the country's natural resources, including what was then cheap and abundant energy. But in the last half century, the discovery and development of more abundant sources of raw materials and energy in other countries eroded U.S. leadership in heavy manufacturing industries that used such inputs intensively. At the same time, the United States became dependent on imports of these same resources, especially petroleum. Thus the fact that our technological progress failed to focus on saving energy and raw materials both made us vulnerable to competitors (like Germany and Japan) who did innovate in those areas, and gave us a chronic trade deficit in natural resource trade (especially oil) which now requires us to run a manufacturing surplus in order to keep overall trade balanced.

At the same time that the U.S. lead in innovative products was undercut, technology transfers and foreign direct investment raised manufacturing productivity levels dramatically in developing countries.

At the same time that the U.S. lead in innovative products was undercut, technology transfers and foreign direct investment raised manufacturing productivity levels dramatically in developing countries and NICs for many types of products (e.g., textiles, apparel, and steel). The rate at which production can be standardized and the technology transferred to low-wage countries has accelerated enormously in the past few decades. The "internationalization of production"—the break-up of the production process into different phases, with the more labor-intensive phases performed in low-wage countries—has contributed to this trend (Fröbel, Heinrichs, and Kreye, 1980). Internationalized production also allows production or assembly of many "high-tech" components to be carried out in low-wage countries, in addition to more traditional products. Since wages in the NICs have remained only a fraction of American wages, the NICs have achieved extraordinary advantages in unit labor costs over the United States in a wide range of manufacturing activities (Mead, 1990).

Thus, the United States' competitive position has been eroded on two fronts. On one hand, the U.S. has lost its monopoly position in more and more high-tech sectors to Japan and other industrialized countries. On the other hand, U.S. productivity advantages in many industrial activities have been substantially reduced, in both low- and high-tech industries, allowing those activities to be transferred to low-wage NICs.

The consequences of these trends for the U.S. standard of living may be interpreted in light of Krugman's (1979) theory of the product cycle in "North-South trade"—i.e., trade between more and less developed regions of the world. In Krugman's model, the North receives monopoly "rents" from its exclusive production of innovative goods.

78

Northern (read American) workers benefit from their nation's monopoly on innovative products by capturing these rents. Northern wages exceed Southern wages in direct proportion to the rate of innovation in the North, and in inverse proportion to the rate at which new products are transferred to the South.

In this framework, the United States suffers from triple jeopardy. First, the rate of innovation seems to be slowing down—not the rate of scientific advance, but the rate at which those advances are commercially applied by domestic producers. Second, due to the entry of other nations into the first ranks of technological leadership, the monopoly rents from the innovation which does take place in the United States are reduced (Soete, 1985). And third, the rate of technology transfer to the South has greatly speeded up. All these factors tend to reduce Northern (U.S.) wages relative to Southern (NIC and LDC) wages, and may even reduce them absolutely.[5]

Given this conceptual framework, the next two chapters will analyze the sources of U.S. trade problems with the individual countries with which the United States has had the largest proportional increases in its trade deficit.

Thus, the United States' competitive position has been eroded on two fronts.

Endnotes

1   Organisation for Economic Co-operation and Development. The OECD includes the U.S., Canada, Australia, New Zealand, most of Southern and Western Europe, and Turkey.

2   The U.S. trade deficit with these regions was reduced principally because the prices of oil and other raw materials which they export fell sharply in the 1980s.

3   Indeed, this argument is not even consistently maintained, as the same report cites the Latin American debt crisis as one of the "macroeconomic" causes of the U.S. trade deficit (p. 97).

4   An important exception, originally noted by Vernon (1966), was innovations designed to economize on the use of natural resources—including energy. Vernon found that West Germany had the lead in this area in the 1960s. This point is discussed further below.

5   More precisely, the equilibrium real wage consistent with balanced trade is reduced; out of equilibrium, if the real wage does not fall sufficiently, the U.S. will have a chronic trade deficit with the South (i.e., the NICs).

Chapter 5.

The Industrialized Surplus Countries: Japan and Germany

Japan and West Germany alone accounted for about half of the U.S. merchandise trade deficit in the late 1980s, although the deficit with Germany was smaller and fell more rapidly than the deficit with Japan. In regard to these countries, the main structural problem is the loss of U.S. dominance in technological innovation. Since U.S. manufactured exports to these countries have traditionally consisted mainly of innovative products, the greater capacity of these nations to produce innovative products on their own erodes the main source of U.S. competitive advantages with them. The fact that these countries were better prepared to meet the challenge of designing energy-saving products and methods of production in the era of high and volatile energy prices also contributed to their heightened competitiveness in the 1970s and 1980s.

In regard to these countries, the main structural problem is the loss of U.S. dominance in technological innovation.

The standard macroeconomic variables—fiscal policies, exchange rates, and saving-investment balances—have also influenced the U.S. trade balance with these nations. But these nations' macro policies and trade performance have not been independent of each other: their macro policies were designed in large part for the goal of fostering competitiveness. Particularly, both Japan and West Germany have used growth strategies which rely more on export markets than on domestic consumers to provide expanding markets for national products.

Technology, Productivity, and Labor Costs

Some evidence on the diminishing gaps in technological leadership between the United States and other industrial countries is given in Table 8 and Figures 11–13. While our main interest is in Japan and West Germany, which have had the largest trade surpluses with the United States, data are also given on other industrialized countries for purposes of comparison. Table 8 shows that the U.S. lead in the proportion of its labor force composed of scientists and engineers engaged in R&D activities was substantially eroded by 1987. Japan had nearly eliminated the gap, while Germany was catching up rapidly. France and the United Kingdom were also catching up, but much more slowly.

The figures given in Table 8 include scientists and engineers working on both defense-related and nondefense R&D. While separate figures for nondefense R&D scientists and engineers are not available, the U.S. proportion would undoubtedly be lower than the Japanese, since about one-third of U.S. R&D expenditures are defense-related while virtually none of the Japanese R&D is defense-related.

Figures 11 and 12 compare U.S. expenditures on R&D as a percentage of GNP with the other four leading industrial nations. In terms of total R&D expenditures (including military), the U.S. is still near the top, while Germany and Japan have just caught up (Figure 11). But since the U.S. devotes the highest percentage of its R&D spending to defense applications, the percentage of nondefense R&D spending in GDP is only about two-thirds of the same percentage in Germany and Japan, and just barely ahead of France and the U.K. (Figure 12).

Another indicator of declining U.S. competitive advantages is the balance of trade in high-tech industries. Figure 13 shows a measure of this balance which includes aircraft

> **The U.S. lead in the proportion of its labor force composed of scientists and engineers engaged in R&D activities was substantially eroded by 1987.**

TABLE 8
Scientists and Engineers Engaged in R&D
Per 10,000 Labor Force, Selected Years and Countries

Year	United States	Japan	West Germany	France	United Kingdom
1965	64.7	24.6	22.6	21.0	19.6
1975	55.3	47.9	38.6	29.2	31.1
1987	75.9	68.8	53.7	44.9	35.9

Source: U.S. National Science Foundation, *National Patterns of R&D Resources: 1990,* NSF Report 90–316, Table B-17, based on data from OECD, U.S. Department of Labor, SRS, and NSF.

Figure 11
National R&D Expenditures as Percent of GNP by Country, 1971-1988

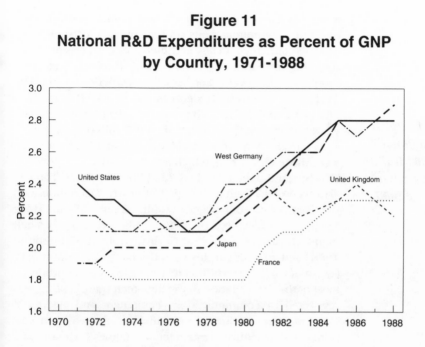

Source: National Science Foundation (1990), Table B-18.

Figure 12
Nondefense R&D Expenditures as Percent of GNP by Country, 1971-1988

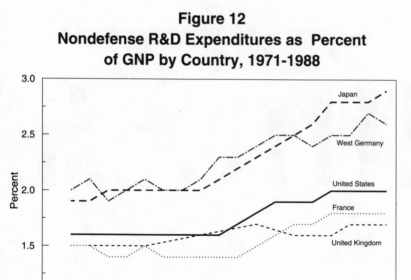

Source: National Science Foundation (1990), Table B-19.

83

and parts, guided missiles and space, computers and office machines, communications equipment and electronic components, ordnance, drugs and medicines, professional and scientific instruments, engines and turbines, industrial inorganic chemicals, and plastics/synthetic resins. The overall U.S. balance of trade in these sectors fell from a surplus of $27 billion in 1980 to a deficit of $1 billion in 1986; it later recovered to a surplus of only $8 billion in 1988.[1]

By far the largest bilateral deficits in high-tech trade were those with Japan, which are also shown in Figure 13. This bilateral deficit reached $22 billion by 1988. The U.S. also recorded a high-tech deficit of nearly $10 billion with the East Asian Four Tigers (South Korea, Taiwan, Hong Kong, and Singapore) by 1988, while retaining a small high-tech surplus with West Germany (about $2 billion in 1988) and a larger surplus with the European Community (EC) as a whole ($16 billion in 1988). In terms of products, most of the deterioration in the high-tech trade balance was registered in communications equipment and electronic components (a decline of $18 billion), followed by professional and scientific instruments, engines/turbines, and

> **By far the largest bilateral deficits in high-tech trade were those with Japan.**

Figure 13
U.S. Trade Balance in High Technology Industries, 1980-88

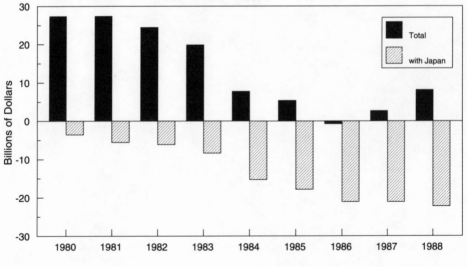

Source: U.S. Department of Commerce, International Trade Administration, Office of Trade and Investment Analysis.

84

office and computing equipment (with declines of about $2 to $3 billion each).

Overall, high-tech trade grew more rapidly than total merchandise trade in the 1980s, but the growth was proportionally more rapid on the import side. Between 1980 and 1988, total nonagricultural exports rose by 56 percent (from $182.9 billion to $285.9 billion), while high-tech exports increased by 91 percent (from $54.7 to $104.3 billion).[2] In the same period, total nonpetroleum merchandise imports more than doubled in value (from $168.2 billion to $410.5 billion, an increase of 144 percent), while *high-tech imports more than tripled* (from $27.3 billion to $96.2 billion, an increase of 251 percent). This more-than-proportional increase in high-tech imports shows that the deterioration in the high-tech trade balance is not merely a reflection of the overall trade deficit or macroeconomic imbalances. It is also consistent with our econometric finding (described in Chapter 3 and the Appendix) that the most significant structural shift in U.S. trade in the 1980s was on the import side, and with the findings of a recent study on U.S. trade with Japan:

The U.S. had the slowest average annual productivity growth rate of any major industrialized nation from 1960 to 1988.

> In the 1970s and the early 80s, capital-intensive manufactures such as household electric machinery, road vehicles, and television sets dominated Japan's exports to the U.S. with a share of more than 60 percent. Reflecting the change in Japan's comparative advantage, these manufactures have been gradually replaced by more technology-intensive products. By 1987 the group of technology-intensive products soared to 40 percent of Japan's total exports to the U.S. from less than 28 percent in 1980.... (Park and Park, 1990, p. 11).

Further indications of the relative decline of U.S. competitiveness compared with other industrialized countries are found in data on productivity and wage growth. Figure 14 shows that the U.S. had the slowest average annual productivity growth rate of any major industrialized nation from 1960 to 1988. Japan was at the top, and West Germany was near the top. Table 9 gives a more detailed breakdown into various subperiods. This breakdown shows that U.S. productivity growth recovered somewhat in the 1980s, while that of some other countries (including West Germany) slowed down. But the United States' recovery was not nearly enough to make up for its relatively sluggish productivity performance in previous decades.

Figure 14
Average Annual Productivity Growth Rates, U.S. and Other Industrial Countries, 1960-1988

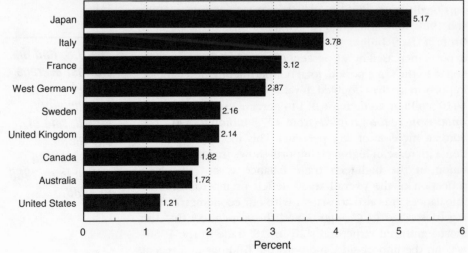

Source: Mishel and Frankel (1991), Table 9.3, based on data from U.S. Department of Labor and OECD.
Note: Average for Australia is for 1967-1988 only.

TABLE 9
Annual Productivity Growth Rates, 1960-88
(in percent)

Country	1960–67	1967–70	1973–79	1979–88	Cumulative 1960–88
Australia	N.A.	2.83%	1.62%	1.06%	1.72%[a]
Canada	2.74%	2.56	1.25	1.30	1.82
France	5.05	4.15	2.40	1.96	3.12
West Germany	4.62	4.25	2.86	1.12	2.87
Italy	7.14	4.99	2.71	1.87	3.78
Japan	9.14	7.74	2.86	2.93	5.17
Sweden	4.71	2.84	0.52	1.35	2.16
United Kingdom	2.70	3.34	1.25	1.79	2.14
United States	3.08	1.03	−0.12	1.09	1.21

Source: Mishel and Frankel (1991), Table 9.3, based on data from U.S. Department of Labor, Bureau of Labor Statistics, and OECD, *National Accounts*, 1990.

Note:
[a]Average for 1967–1988 only.

As the U.S. lead in productivity was eroded by more rapid productivity growth abroad, the U.S. lost its absolute productivity advantages in many individual sectors. For example, Szirmai and Pilat (1990) found that Japan had surpassed the United States absolutely in labor productivity (gross value per hour worked) by 1985 in three key sectors: basic and fabricated metal products, machinery and transport equipment, and electrical machinery and equipment. Dollar and Wolff (1988), using a different methodology, found that the United States retained an absolute productivity advantage in only ten of twenty-eight manufacturing industries studied as of 1982. In the other eighteen industries, the advantage had passed to Italy (nine, mostly light industries), the U.K. (four), Japan, Austria, France, Australia, and West Germany (one each).

U.S. wages have been falling relative to wages in other industrialized countries, and even in absolute terms by some measures.

The loss of the U.S. relative and, in some cases, absolute advantages in technology and productivity implies that the U.S. can only hope to maintain balanced trade by lowering its wages and/or depreciating the dollar. In fact, U.S. wages have been falling relative to wages in other industrialized countries, and even in absolute terms by some measures (corrected for inflation). Figure 15 compares the growth of real hourly compensation of manufacturing workers (both production workers and all employees) in the U.S. and other industrialized countries for 1979–1988. The U.S. is clearly in last place for growth of production workers' compensation, as the U.S. is the only country which recorded a *decrease* in this category over the nine-year period 1979–1988.[3] The U.S. is only second-to-last in all employees' compensation, as positive compensation growth among professional and supervisory workers more than compensated for the negative compensation growth among production workers (although not by much). The fact that the U.S. trade deficit increased so dramatically while U.S. wages were falling relatively and (for production workers) even absolutely suggests a particularly severe competitiveness problem (Hatsopoulos et al., 1988).

The fact that U.S. wages have been falling is important for rebutting the popular notion that high wages, especially in unionized industries, are responsible for the problems of American competitiveness. A recent study by Karier (1990) has shown that this notion is a fallacy, both at the aggregate level and at the industry level. The U.S. labor force is actually much less unionized than the labor forces in most other industrialized countries. After controlling for

Figure 15
Average Annual Growth Rates of Real Hourly Manufacturing Compensation, 1979-1988

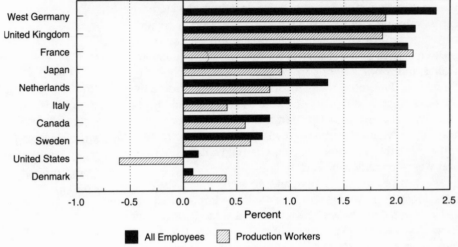

Source: Hourly compensation in national currency from U.S. Department of Labor, BLS; deflated by CPI's from IMF, International Financial Statistics (1989).

The U.S. has tended to become more competitive with other industrialized countries in terms of unit labor costs.

certain industry characteristics, Karier shows that there is no statistically significant correlation between unionization and imports, exports, or net exports at the industry level.

In fact, the U.S. has tended to become *more* competitive with other industrialized countries in terms of *unit labor costs* (wages divided by output per hour, or wages relative to productivity), for most of the last two decades. Table 10 and Figure 16 show indexes of U.S. unit labor costs relative to a trade-weighted average of the unit labor costs for ten other countries (Canada, Japan, and most of Western Europe) in manufacturing from 1970 to 1989. Measured in terms of national currencies, relative U.S. unit labor costs have fallen for most of the last two decades, except for a brief rise toward the end of the 1970s. When foreign unit labor costs are converted to dollars at prevailing exchange rates, the decline is continuous from 1970 to 1980. But relative U.S. unit labor costs in U.S. dollars shot up between 1980 and 1985—not because U.S. workers received higher wages, but because the dollar rose sharply in value (which made other countries' wages cheaper in dollar terms). Once the dollar fell after 1985, relative U.S. unit labor costs

TABLE 10
U.S. Unit Labor Costs in Manufacturing Relative to
Other Industrialized Countries, 1973–1989
(Indexes, 1973 = 100)

	National Currency Basis	U.S. Dollar Basis
1973	100.0	100.0
1980	95.4	88.9
1985	92.1	124.3
1989	81.3	76.5

Source: U.S. Department of Labor, BLS, Office of Productivity and Technology, April 1991, unpublished data.

Note: The indexes are ratios of the U.S. index to a trade-weighted geometric average of the indexes for Canada, Japan, and Europe.

Figure 16
U.S. Manufacturing Unit Labor Costs Relative to
Other Industrialized Countries, 1970-1989

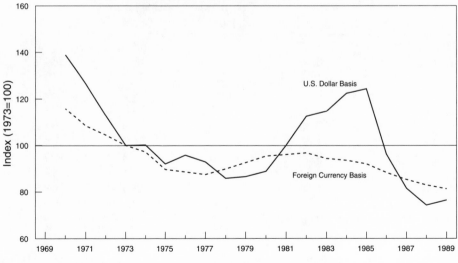

Source: U.S. Department of Labor, BLS, Office of Productivity and Technology, April 1991.
Note: Other industrialized countries include Canada, Japan, and Europe.

resumed their downward trend, reaching a record low in 1989. *The fact that the U.S. has had recurrent trade problems with other industrialized countries*—especially Japan and Germany—*in spite of secularly falling relative unit labor costs indicates that U.S. competitive problems do not result from high wages.*

Indeed, in terms of unit labor costs, it would appear that the United States has become a low-wage country, at least among the industrialized nations. Confirmation of this point comes from a study by Hooper and Larin (1989). Hooper and Larin compare *absolute* unit labor costs in dollars across countries, with outputs measured at "purchasing power parity" exchange rates (in constant 1980 dollars), and wages (hourly compensation) converted at market exchange rates. As shown in Table 11, this comparison shows that the U.S. had lower unit labor costs than most other industrialized nations in 1987.[4] This confirms that the large U.S. deficits of the 1980s, especially those with Japan and Germany, cannot be blamed on high unit labor costs in the United States.

TABLE 11
Unit Labor Costs in Manufacturing, 1987
(in U.S. dollars, except as noted)

Country	Hourly Compensation	Output per Hour[a]	Unit Labor Costs[b]	Percent of U.S.
United States	$13.46	$19.5	68.8¢	100.0%
West Germany	16.83	14.9	113.3	164.7
Japan	11.34	13.9	81.8	118.9
France	12.36	14.9	82.7	120.2
United Kingdom	9.07	10.1	90.2	131.1
Italy	12.33	18.4	66.9	97.2
Canada	11.98	16.7	71.6	104.1
Belgium	15.08	20.0	75.3	109.4
Netherlands	15.11	18.4	82.1	119.3
South Korea	1.69	5.3	32.0	46.5

Source: Hooper and Larin (1989).

Notes:
[a]Real manufacturing output at constant 1980 prices, converted to U.S. dollars using purchasing power parity exchange rates, per hour of employed workers.
[b]In U.S. cents per unit of output (hourly compensation divided by output per hour).

Macro Policies and Exchange Rates

The structural deterioration in the U.S. trade position relative to other industrialized countries defines the environment in which the macro policy changes of the 1980s were played out. However, those policies also had independent effects which determined the precise course of bilateral trade imbalances over the decade. When we bring the macro policies into the picture, two conclusions emerge: (1) the way macro policies influenced the trade deficit was different in the cases of West Germany and Japan; and (2) the bilateral deficit with Japan seems to have been more structural, as it was much less responsive to exchange rate adjustments.

Figures 17 and 18 show the value of the dollar relative to the West German deutschemark (DM) and Japanese yen (¥) in both nominal and real (inflation-adjusted) terms, respectively, since 1979. The value of the dollar in DM follows the same general pattern in the 1980s as the overall value of the dollar shown in Figures 3 and 8: it rose sharply in 1980–85, and then fell even more quickly in 1985–88, both in nominal and real terms. Note also how closely the DM/$ exchange rate follows the U.S.-German interest rate differential graphed in Figure 5.[5] But the dollar's movements against the Yen are quite different. *There was no sharp appreciation of the dollar against the yen in the early 1980s*, in either nominal or real terms. The ¥/$ exchange rate had only a slight upward trend from 1979 to 1985 in real terms, and no trend in nominal terms.

Figure 19 shows the bilateral merchandise trade balances with West Germany and Japan for the last decade. The deficit with West Germany basically rose and fell with the DM/$ exchange rate, allowing for a lag of about two years (the dollar peaked in 1985 and the deficit in 1987). However, while the U.S.-Japanese bilateral deficit rose rapidly from 1982 to 1987, the dollar did *not* rise very much against the yen in 1980–85. And this deficit persisted at $41 billion in 1990 in spite of a virtual collapse of the dollar against the yen after 1985. Clearly, *the dramatic increase in the bilateral U.S.-Japan deficit in the early 1980s cannot be attributed to the exchange rate, and exchange rate adjustment was relatively ineffective in reducing the U.S.-Japanese bilateral deficit in the late 1980s.*

> *The dramatic increase in the bilateral U.S.-Japan deficit in the early 1980s cannot be attributed to the exchange rate.*

91

Figure 17
German Deutschemarks and Japanese Yen per Dollar, Quarterly 1979-1990

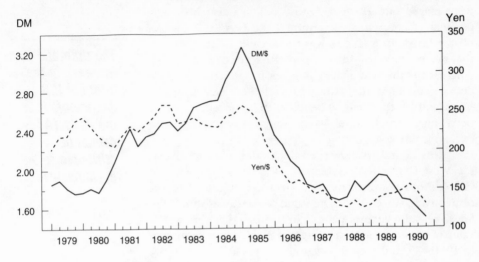

Source: Federal Reserve Board of Governors.

Figure 18
Real German and Japanese Exchange Rates, Quarterly 1979-1990

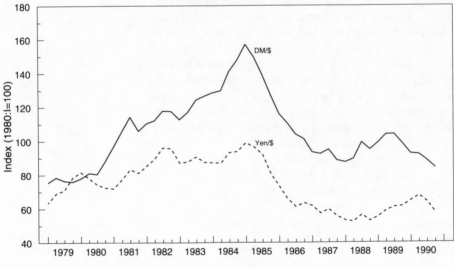

Sources: Federal Reserve Board of Governors and Department of Labor, BLS.
Note: Real exchange rates were calculated using consumer price indexes.

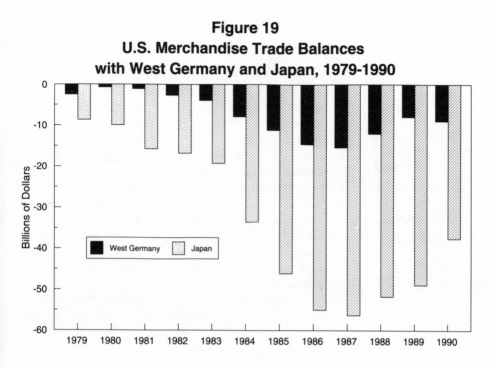

Figure 19
U.S. Merchandise Trade Balances
with West Germany and Japan, 1979-1990

The U.S. trade deficit with Germany is thus neither as large nor as intractable as that with Japan. The German trade surplus with the U.S. has been much more responsive to exchange rate adjustment. And while the situation may change in the 1990s as a result of European economic integration, West Germany by itself does not yet pose as great a challenge to U.S. technological leadership as Japan. For this reason, the rest of this section will focus on Japanese macro policies.

The macroeconomic causes of the U.S.-Japan deficit can best be understood in terms of the changes in the saving-investment and government budget balances shown in Table 1. First, as discussed earlier, the simultaneous pursuit of opposite fiscal policies—contractionary in Japan and expansionary in the U.S.—contributed to large trade imbalances. In addition, Japan reduced its gross private domestic fixed investment more than it reduced its private saving (3.0 versus 2.5 percent of GDP), while the U.S. reduced its domestic investment by the same amount as it reduced saving (0.8 percent of GDP). The sharp decline in the aggregate Japanese domestic investment rate, combined with the

> *The U.S. trade deficit with Germany is thus neither as large nor as intractable as that with Japan.*

93

tightening of fiscal policy, created a large pool of excess domestic savings which was used to finance Japan's growing trade surplus and net foreign investment.

As pointed out in a staff study by the Joint Economic Committee (U.S. Congress, 1988), the overall decline in the Japanese investment rate masks some important compositional shifts. According to this study, "Despite the drop in overall investment, however, real investment in the manufacturing sector expanded rapidly" (p. 15), while housing investment fell (as a percentage of GNP). The reduction in housing investment was precipitated by "the reduction or elimination of several government programs to assist private investment in housing" (p. 16). In addition, the government cut public investment spending significantly in the early 1980s, which accounted for a large part of the fiscal tightening. Since the price of manufacturing plant and equipment rose more slowly than average prices, "The sharp increase in real [manufacturing] investment laid the basis for more exports, while the smaller increase in nominal [total] investment meant that there was more savings available for investment abroad" (p. 17).

The policy and behavioral changes in Japan must be viewed in the context of important differences in the structure and operation of Japanese economic institutions compared with their American counterparts. These structural differences have been analyzed in depth by Johnson (1982) and Prestowitz (1988), among others, and a full discussion of them would be beyond the scope of this report. The point to be emphasized here is how these structural differences have interacted with the macroeconomic climate to produce a tendency toward persistent trade surpluses.

There are two closely related features of the Japanese economy which are relevant in this regard (see Salvatore, 1990, for an excellent survey). One is the active use of industrial and trade policies to promote the development of a sequence of strategic economic sectors: first basic industries such as steel, then consumer durables industries such as automobiles, and now high-technology sectors such as semiconductors. The other is the relative closure of the Japanese market to imports, especially of manufactured products—partly as a byproduct of strategic industrial targeting, and partly as an effect of domestic market institutions (e.g., the well-known difficulties in penetrating the domestic distribution system). Dornbusch (1990, p. 121) cites figures showing that Japan's imports of manufac-

> **Japan's imports of manufactures have stayed constant at about 2 percent of its GNP since the late 1960s.**

tures have stayed constant at about 2 percent of its GNP since the late 1960s, while U.S. imports of manufactures have risen to about 6 percent of GNP in 1988 (from less than 2 percent in 1967). The closed character of the Japanese market for manufactures has also been documented by Lawrence (1987), who found that Japan's imports of manufactures are about 40 percent lower than one would expect from that country's economic characteristics.

The key question is how such structural factors could have contributed to Japan's trade surpluses. Many economists (e.g., Krueger, 1990) have argued that the Japanese trade surpluses of the last decade cannot logically be explained by these structural factors, since Japanese industrial policies and trade barriers were no higher in the 1980s than in the past, and if anything the Japanese economy had been liberalized to some extent. Certainly, it would be factually and logically incorrect to ascribe the Japanese trade surpluses to *increased* trade barriers or industrial targeting in the 1980s. Nevertheless, there are two ways in which *existing* structural trade barriers and industrial policies could have affected Japan's trade balance.

There are two ways in which existing structural trade barriers and industrial policies could have affected Japan's trade balance.

First, Japanese industrial policy and corporate planning have succeeded in moving Japanese industry "upscale" technologically. Japan has become competitive with the United States not only in traditional "smokestack" industries such as autos and steel, but also in "high tech" areas such as capital goods, electronic products, and computers. Thus Japan has come to have an enormous structural surplus with the United States in the trade of manufactures, a surplus which cannot realistically be offset by U.S. exports of primary products and services under present conditions (especially since the Japanese agricultural and service sectors are also largely closed to imports). This structural surplus in manufacturing is not due to increased trade barriers or industrial targeting, but rather to the *cumulative* effects of *past* as well as present policies.

Second, Japan's structural impediments to imports acquire increased significance in the context of the changing macroeconomic environment described above. As discussed in relation to Table 4, Cline (1989, p. 155) estimated that the income elasticity of U.S. import demand (the percentage by which imports increase, when domestic income rises by 1 percent) is 2.44, while the income elasticity of U.S. export demand (the percentage by which exports increase, when foreign income rises by 1 percent) is only 1.70. The analogous elasticities for Japan are 1.21 for imports and 2.24 for exports.[6] As a result, when the U.S. expanded its domestic demand while Japan contracted its domestic demand in the early 1980s, U.S. imports of Japanese products rose relatively rapidly. When Japan grew more rapidly at the end of the decade, Japanese imports from the U.S. did pick up, but not nearly enough to offset the already high level of U.S. imports from Japan.

This last point is so often ignored in studies of the trade deficit which focus only on macro policies that it cannot be emphasized too strongly. *A nation's structural characteristics determine the parameters which in turn determine how changes in macro policies (at home and abroad) affect its trade balance.* If Japan were less closed to imports, or the U.S. were less open, then the same fiscal policies in the U.S. and Japan might result in a smaller trade imbalance. This is precisely why there is no logical fallacy in insisting that structural differences between countries can affect their trade balance, even though that balance is a macroeconomic variable.

To be sure, there have been some improvements in the U.S.-Japan bilateral trade imbalance as a result of the post-1985 dollar depreciation. The dollar value of U.S. exports to Japan more than doubled from $23 billion in 1985 to $48 billion in 1990.[7] However, due to the depreciation of the dollar from ¥238 in 1985 to ¥145 in 1990, Japanese *expenditures* on imports from the U.S. in yen terms rose by a much smaller proportion than the dollar value of U.S. exports to Japan, from ¥5.4 trillion in 1985 to ¥7.0 trillion in 1990 (an increase of only about 30 percent). And U.S. imports from Japan continued to grow from $69 billion to a peak of $94 billion in 1989, before declining to $90 billion in 1990 (as the U.S. economy went into a recession). Although the proportional increase in exports to Japan was much greater, the absolute increase in imports was almost as large since imports started from a higher base. As a result, the bilateral deficit fell only to $41 billion in 1990, just slightly below the 1985 deficit of $46 billion.

One reason for the continued growth of U.S. imports was that Japanese firms preferred to reduce their profit margins instead of raising the dollar prices of their exports in order to maintain their market share in the U.S. This has come to be known as the limited "pass through" of dollar depreciation into import prices (Mann, 1986; Hooper and Mann, 1989a; Marston, 1990). Moreover, to the extent that Japa-

If Japan were less closed to imports, or the U.S. were less open, then the same fiscal policies in the U.S. and Japan might result in a smaller trade imbalance.

96

nese commercial success is due to absolute technological advances and perceived quality advantages, consumers would not necessarily abandon Japanese products even if their prices increased.

A tactic that the Japanese have used to try to reduce their bilateral trade surplus with the U.S. while maintaining their markets here is to shift their strategy from exports to direct foreign investment. To the extent that such investment is made in the U.S. (as opposed to Mexico or southeast Asia), such investment could potentially improve the U.S. trade balance. This would be especially true if the foreign-owned plants would produce for export. In practice, however, the benefits for U.S. trade may be negligible or even negative since Japanese foreign subsidiaries tend to have very high propensities to import capital goods and intermediate products from their parent companies in Japan (Kreinin, 1988; Graham and Krugman, 1989). Also, to the extent that Japanese firms invest in "offshore" production facilities in "export platforms" in less developed countries such as Thailand and Mexico, Japan can reduce its *bilateral* surplus with the U.S. without reducing the *overall* U.S. trade deficit.

Japanese foreign subsidiaries tend to have very high propensities to import capital goods and intermediate products from their parent companies in Japan.

Endnotes

[1] All data on high-tech trade in this and the following paragraphs are from U.S. Department of Commerce, International Trade Administration, Office of Trade and Investment Analysis. Comparable data for 1989 and 1990 are not available yet due to ongoing reclassifications of the data.

[2] All data in this paragraph are in current dollars.

[3] The extent of the decline in U.S. real compensation may be exaggerated slightly by the use of the official consumer price index (CPI), which is based on different treatments of housing costs before and after 1983, and which is generally regarded as overestimating these costs in 1979–1983 (when they were measured by purchase price instead of rental equivalent). However, U.S. real compensation would still have fallen (for production workers) even if another measure of consumer prices, such as the fixed weight index for personal consumption expenditures from the NIPAs, were used. See Mishel and Frankel (1991), Table 9.1 and Figure 9B, which uses the latter measure. The CPI is used here for consistency with other countries. The U.S. rate would still be negative if the data were extended to 1990, but comparable data for other countries are not yet available.

[4] Hooper and Larin's calculations can be criticized on the basis of the problems with the U.S. data on real manufacturing output (value-added) noted by Mishel (1988). Mishel argues that value-added in manufacturing in constant dollars was exaggerated in the early 1980s by the methods used to deflate nominal value added. I have calculated that making the adjustments to the U.S. data suggested by Mishel would raise U.S. unit labor costs for 1987 only to $73.2, which would not affect any of the qualitative conclusions drawn here from Hooper and Larin's data. Only Canada would shift to having unit labor costs lower than the U.S.

[5] Not coincidentally, one of the studies which found the largest effects of the U.S. budget deficit on the rise of the dollar in the early 1980s (Feldstein, 1986) focused solely on the DM/$ exchange rate.

[6] For direct, bilateral trade between the U.S. and Japan, Cline found that the elasticity of U.S. exports to Japan with respect to Japanese income was 1.229. His estimate of the elasticity of Japanese exports to the U.S. with respect to U.S. income was higher than 3.0 (his upper constraint on income-elasticities in his model). See his Table 4A.2, p. 172.

[7] The data in this paragraph are from U.S. Department of Commerce, Bureau of Economic Analysis, *Business Statistics, 1961–88,* and *Survey of Current Business*, February, 1991.

Chapter 6.

Trade Problems with Developing Countries

Low-Wage Exporters of Manufactures

U.S. trade problems with the newly industrializing countries (NICs) are of a different nature from its problems with Japan and Germany today. To be sure, the NICs—especially the so-called Four Tigers (South Korea, Taiwan, Singapore, and Hong Kong)—have imitated the Japanese strategy of relying on export markets rather than domestic demand to fuel their growth. But these countries are relatively less industrially developed, with real wages and living standards far below those prevailing in the U.S. and other industrialized countries. By importing relatively advanced technology for producing standardized products (e.g., textiles, steel, and basic automobiles), the leading NICs have been able to combine high productivity with low wages in order to obtain significant absolute advantages in unit labor costs (Mead, 1990).

The leading NICs have been able to combine high productivity with low wages in order to obtain significant absolute advantages in unit labor costs.

To begin with, it is worth examining the available statistics on how much lower wages are in developing countries. Table 12 gives indexes of hourly compensation costs for production workers in manufacturing relative to U.S. costs, converted to dollars at prevailing exchange rates, for selected developing countries ranked according to their compensation levels in 1975. It should be kept in mind that most of these countries for which the U.S. Department of Labor is able to obtain data are among the better-off developing countries, and that these are averages for all manufacturing industries which conceal considerable divergences at the industry level (especially between protected import-substitution sectors and competitive export sectors).

The compensation costs ranged from a low of 4 percent of the U.S. level in Sri Lanka to a high of 31 percent in Mexico[1] in 1975. In the 1980s, wages in the successful East Asian NICs (Hong Kong, Singapore, Korea, and Taiwan) rose impressively relative to the U.S., although none exceeded one-quarter of U.S. compensation by 1989. At the same time, wages in the Latin American debtor nations fell dramatically, to 16 percent of the U.S. in Mexico[2] and 12 percent in Brazil. Meanwhile, from the scarce data available (on Sri Lanka), it appears that the poorest South Asian countries stayed behind at abysmally low wage levels. Unfortunately, comparable data are not available on Southeast Asian exporters such as Thailand and Malaysia, but they would probably fall somewhere between South Asia and Latin America.

The idea that low wages can confer absolute competitive advantages on a country is routinely dismissed by international economists on *a priori* theoretical grounds. For example, Lawrence and Litan assert:

> ... since wage levels tend to reflect productivity levels, high-wage countries such as the United States *can* compete with low-wage countries because their superior productivity compensates for higher wage rates. If developing countries really had U.S. skills, technology, and capital levels, their wages would no longer be low. (1987, p. 290)

This statement would be perfectly logical *if* low wages in developing countries merely compensated for lower productivity. But the assertion that low wages *actually do* just compensate for lower productivity is not backed up by any data. Low-wage countries today do not generally have productivity levels so low as to eliminate their competitive advantages in most manufactured goods.[3]

The traditional view that low wages cannot lead to absolute competitive advantages is based on the classical (Ricardian) theory of international trade (see, e.g., Krugman and Obstfeld, 1988, Chapter 2). This theory assumes that the productivity of labor in each country is independently given by its natural resources, labor skills, and technological capabilities. The theory also assumes a perfectly competitive labor market, in which the wage level necessarily settles at the average productivity of labor for the economy

The assertion that low wages actually do just compensate for lower productivity is not backed up by any data.

100

TABLE 12
Hourly Compensation Costs for Manufacturing Production Workers, Selected Years and Countries, as Percent of U.S.

	1975	1980	1985	1989
United States	100	100	100	100
Mexico	31	30	16	16[a]
Brazil	14	14	9	12
Hong Kong	12	15	13	19
Singapore	13	15	19	22
South Korea	6	10	10	25
Taiwan	6	10	12	25
Sri Lanka	4	2	2	2[b]

Source: U.S. Department of Labor, Bureau of Labor Statistics, Office of Productivity and Technology. "International Comparisons of Hourly Compensation Costs for Production Workers in Manufacturing, 1975–89," Report 794, October 1990a.

Notes:
[a]Preliminary estimate.
[b]Figure is for 1987.

as a whole.[4] In this case, the country will have comparative advantages in those commodities in which its relative productivity (compared with foreign productivity) is greater than the country's relative wage level (compared with foreign wages). Correspondingly, the country will have comparative disadvantages in those commodities in which its relative productivity is less than the relative wage. If wages freely adjust to equalize the demand for labor with the supply, trade will be exactly balanced.

There are two problems in applying this doctrine to today's NICs. First, technology and capital are internationally mobile, enabling less developed countries to raise their productivity levels far above what their domestic technological capabilities alone would permit. Second, these countries suffer from what development economists have called "dualism" in labor markets (see, e.g., Todaro, 1989). That is, developing countries typically have a modern capitalist sector which uses advanced technology alongside a backward subsistence sector which uses traditional methods (sometimes called the "informal sector"). They also have a surplus of labor in the subsistence sector, which is willing to work in the modern sector for relatively low wages.

Technology and capital are internationally mobile.

101

This segmentation of labor markets implies that they are *not* perfectly competitive, and that wages do *not* freely adjust to equalize the total demand for labor with the supply in the modern sector where there is chronic excess supply. Wages do tend to be somewhat higher in the modern sector than in the rest of the economy, but they are still constrained by the ever-present competition of impoverished workers from the subsistence or informal sector seeking better-paying jobs in the modern sector.

The possibility of a persistent competitive advantage arises because the modern capitalist sector generally produces tradeable goods for the international market, while the traditional subsistence sector often produces mainly for the domestic market. Thus wages tend to be low relative to productivity in tradeable goods (chiefly manufactures) more or less across the board. Of course, these countries will not be able to export all internationally traded goods; they must still import innovative and high-tech products from the advanced countries, as well as raw materials and energy resources not available domestically. But they will have a persistent advantage in unit labor costs in a wide spectrum of manufacturing activities.

Mead (1990) gives some examples of this phenomenon. He cites figures showing that the Brazilian and Korean steel industries have productivity levels about 60 percent of U.S. levels, while their wages are only about 10 percent of U.S. wages. As a result, their unit labor costs are only about one-sixth of U.S. unit labor costs in steel production (p. 16). In shirt making, Hong Kong and South Korea can produce a men's shirt at less than one-third of the American unit abor cost ($0.46 per shirt in Hong Kong and $0.53 in Korea, compared with $1.76 in the U.S.)—and still poorer countries have even lower unit labor costs, less than one-tenth of American costs ($0.14 in Sri Lanka, $0.15 in India, and $0.10 in Bangladesh).

Two recent studies have attempted to compare U.S. and South Korean productivity for manufacturing as a whole. According to Hooper and Larin (1989), South Korea had unit labor costs which were less than half of the U.S. in 1987 (see Table 11, above). Based on their estimates, Korean productivity is *not* low enough to compensate for its low wages in *the entire manufacturing sector* (which accounts for most of Korea's trade—over 90 percent of its exports).

*Labor markets
. . . are not
perfectly
competitive, and
. . . wages do
not freely adjust
to equalize the
total demand for
labor with the
supply.*

The estimates of Szirmai and Pilat (1990) show Korean productivity to be slightly lower, compared to the United States, than it appears in Hooper and Larin's study. Szirmai and Pilat (p. 28) find that Korean value-added per hour worked in manufacturing had reached just 19 percent of the U.S. level using U.S. quantity weights, and only 11 percent using Korean weights, in 1985, compared with 23 percent in the same year according to Hooper and Larin. However, since Korean hourly compensation of manufacturing production workers was only 10 percent of the U.S. rate in 1985 (see Table 12), Korea still had systematically lower unit labor costs for manufacturing, at least when those costs are calculated using U.S. quantity weights. And these weights would seem to be more appropriate for international competition, since the U.S. quantities are more reflective of conditions in the markets to which Korea exports.

By 1984 Mexican productivity was about 60–80 percent of U.S. productivity.

The problem of systematically lower unit labor costs in manufacturing is not limited to East Asia. Blomstrom and Wolff (1989) found that Mexican labor productivity (value-added per employee) in all manufacturing had reached nearly half of U.S. productivity by 1970, and remained about half in 1975. In 1975, however, Mexican hourly compensation in manufacturing was less than one-third of U.S. compensation ($2.00 versus $6.36, according to U.S. Department of Labor, BLS, 1989, p. 572)—and that was with an overvalued peso that was devalued the following year, and while Mexican industries were still heavily protected by import substitution policies. To obtain more recent data, Blomstrom and Wolff had to use a different data source which did not allow them to calculate an average for all manufacturing. Nevertheless, they found that by 1984 Mexican productivity was about 60–80 percent of U.S. productivity in most of the industries for which comparable data was available. By that time, however, Mexican compensation had actually fallen to about 16 percent of U.S. compensation (same source), resulting in an even greater unit labor cost advantage. And compensation in Mexico's export-oriented maquiladoras are only about half of the official national average for domestic manufacturing.

Similar results were obtained by Maddison and van Ark (1989). They put average Mexican labor productivity in manufacturing in 1975 at 45 percent of the U.S. level using U.S. quantity weights, although it was only 33 percent using Mexican weights. They also found that average Brazilian labor productivity in manufacturing was 59 percent of the U.S. level in 1975 using U.S. quantity weights and 42 percent using Brazilian weights; Brazilian wages were only 14 percent of U.S. at that time (U.S. Department of Labor, BLS, 1990a).

Taiwan and South Korea have pursued export-oriented development strategies since the 1960s.

While low unit labor costs give a country a competitive advantage, the extent to which such an advantage translates into a trade surplus depends on other factors, primarily macroeconomic policies. Macro policies can help to offset competitive advantages in unit labor costs, either by allowing the currency to appreciate or by stimulating import demand, thus keeping trade balanced. Alternatively, macro policies can either fail to offset competitive advantages or even exacerbate them, thus fostering chronic trade surpluses. The way in which macro policies have contributed to the problem has varied between the East Asian NICs (particularly South Korea and Taiwan) and the Latin American debtors (especially Mexico and Brazil). We now turn to examine each of these cases.

The East Asian NICs: Undervalued Currencies and Export-Led Growth

The successful East Asian NICs have followed a development strategy known as "export-led growth." In this strategy, the country relies on expanding exports to foreign countries to provide the demand for growing domestic industries. This strategy does not necessarily entail trade surpluses, if the growth of exports is matched by the growth of imports. But chronic trade surpluses can result if import demand lags behind. In this case, export-led (or rather, trade surplus-driven) growth becomes a "beggar-thy-neighbor" policy, which effectively exports unemployment to other nations (those with trade deficits). This outcome can occur if domestic demand is restrained through a combination of low wages (relative to productivity), conservative fiscal policies, and incentives for individuals to save rather than to consume. Trade barriers which keep the domestic market closed to imports can also contribute to chronic trade surpluses in a country with highly competitive exports.

Although Taiwan and South Korea have pursued export-oriented development strategies since the 1960s, these countries did not develop large trade surpluses with the United States until the late 1970s (in the case of Taiwan) and the mid-1980s (in the case of Korea). Although Korean and Taiwanese exports rose very rapidly in the 1960s and 1970s, their imports grew at least as fast. In addition to importing raw materials and energy products, South Korea and Taiwan had to import a large portion of the capital goods required for investment in their growing industries—and they bought significant shares of these goods from the United States.

In the 1980s, however, two changes occurred. First, South Korea and Taiwan began to import a higher share of their capital goods from Japan (Park and Park, 1990). This allowed Korea and Taiwan to move into trade deficits with Japan at the same time that they developed large surpluses with the United States. Second, as Korea and Taiwan developed industrially, they became less dependent on imported capital goods. Since imports of consumer goods were still highly restricted, in spite of some liberalization efforts, the reduced imports of capital goods were not replaced by increased imports of consumer goods (Moreno, 1989). As a result, import growth began to lag behind export growth, and overall trade surpluses arose (a few years after the bilateral surpluses with the U.S. in each case).

In spite of some liberalization efforts, the reduced imports of capital goods were not replaced by increased imports of consumer good.

As noted in the discussion of competitiveness in Chapter 1, competitive advantages (including those due to low unit labor costs) can potentially be offset by a sufficient appreciation of a nation's currency. The behavior of the Korean and Taiwanese exchange rates has been analyzed in studies by Moreno (1989) and the U.S. General Accounting Office (1989). Both Korea and Taiwan have managed exchange rates. The Bank of Korea (BOK) administers the value of the won on a daily basis. Since the Korean won is not freely traded, the BOK can control the won exchange rate without massive intervention in foreign exchange markets. The Taiwan dollar, on the other hand, is regulated by a managed float. This requires continuous intervention which is directed by the Central Bank of China through two surrogates, the Bank of Taiwan and the International Commercial Bank of China.

As Figure 20 shows, the Korean won depreciated substantially in nominal terms from 1980 to 1985, and in real terms from 1982 to 1986. This depreciation was consciously intended to improve Korea's international competitiveness in order to reverse the trade deficits of the late 1970s. Moreno (1989) found that the depreciation of the won was the main proximate cause of Korea's dramatic shift from a trade deficit to a trade surplus in the 1980s. In this respect, Korea's exchange rate policy helped to reinforce rather than to offset the country's increasing competitive advantages in unit labor costs. Starting in 1986, under considerable pressure from the United States, Korea began to let the won appreciate—although continued domestic inflation meant that the real appreciation was less than the nominal appreciation. In real terms, the won in 1989 was still nearly 10 percent below its 1982 peak. And the won depreciated again in 1990, in both nominal and real terms.

The depreciation of the won in the early 1980s reinforced, rather than offset, Korea's tendency toward competitive advantages in unit labor costs.

Table 13 shows how the depreciation of the won in the early 1980s reinforced, rather than offset, Korea's tendency toward competitive advantages in unit labor costs. From 1981 to 1986, Korea's unit labor costs actually *fell* about 15 percent in U.S. dollar terms. This fall is entirely attributable to the depreciation of the won, since Korean unit labor costs in national currency rose about 9 percent over the same period. After 1986, however, the appreciation of the won led to a dramatic reversal, with Korean unit labor costs rising much more in dollar terms than in won terms (about 75 percent versus 33 percent from 1986–89).

Figure 20
Nominal and Real Effective Exchange Rates of the Korean Won, 1981-1990

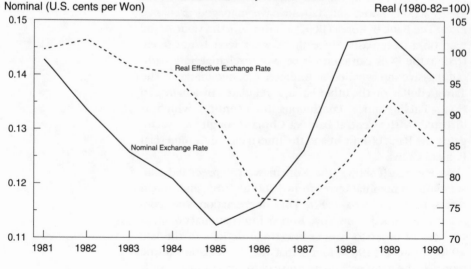

Sources: GAO report NSIAD-89-130; Morgan Guaranty Trust Company; IMF, *International Financial Statistics.*

The situation in Taiwan was similar in outcome, but with different mechanisms at work. As Figure 21 shows, the Taiwan dollar fell sharply in real terms from 1981 to 1986, but depreciated relatively little in nominal terms against the U.S. dollar. This discrepancy is explained by Taiwan's very low inflation rate, which allowed its real competitiveness to improve without a major nominal depreciation. Nevertheless, the Taiwanese monetary authorities did intervene substantially to prevent the Taiwan dollar from appre-

TABLE 13
Korean and Taiwanese Unit Labor Costs, 1970–1989
(Indexes, 1982 = 100)

Year	Korea National Currency	Korea U.S. Dollars	Taiwan National Currency	Taiwan U.S. Dollars
1970	15.4	36.3	30.0	29.4
1971	16.4	34.5	31.6	30.9
1972	18.2	33.8	32.0	31.3
1973	21.6	39.7	37.3	38.1
1974	26.8	48.4	56.3	58.0
1975	30.7	46.4	57.0	58.7
1976	38.8	58.6	59.0	60.8
1977	45.2	68.3	61.6	63.4
1978	54.0	81.5	62.3	65.8
1979	65.4	98.8	70.8	76.8
1980	82.8	99.7	81.4	88.4
1981	95.1	102.1	93.9	99.7
1982	100.0	100.0	100.0	100.0
1983	105.6	99.6	98.7	96.3
1984	106.3	96.4	102.9	101.7
1985	105.4	88.6	106.8	104.9
1986	104.0	86.3	110.0	113.7
1987	109.3	97.2	110.0	135.6
1988	121.5	121.5	113.5	155.1
1989	138.1	150.4	118.4	175.4

Source: U.S. Department of Labor, Bureau of Labor Statistics, "International Comparisons of Manufacturing Productivity and Labor Cost Trends, 1989," July 1990b.

ciating as a result of the country's growing trade surpluses in the early and mid-1980s (Moreno, 1989).

In order to prevent a currency from appreciating when there is an excess inflow of foreign exchange (at the prevailing exchange rate), a central bank has to buy up the excess foreign currency. The purchased foreign exchange then adds to the accumulated reserves of the central bank. For this reason, Taiwan's extraordinary accumulation of international reserves provides strong evidence of its central bank's intervention to keep the Taiwan dollar undervalued. As of the end of 1989, Taiwan had foreign exchange reserves (excluding gold) valued at $73 billion, larger than the reserves of any other country in the world except Japan[5]—and this was *after* the Taiwan dollar had been allowed to appreciate by about 50 percent (in nominal terms) from 1985 to 1989.

As in the case of Korea, the appreciation of the Taiwanese currency in the late 1980s was not an automatic response to market pressures, but rather a conscious response to political pressures from the United States. In fact, the real appreciation of the Taiwan dollar has been greater than that

Taiwan's extraordinary accumulation of international reserves provides strong evidence of its central bank's intervention to keep the Taiwan dollar undervalued.

Figure 21
Nominal and Real Effective Exchange Rates of
the New Taiwan Dollar, 1981-1990

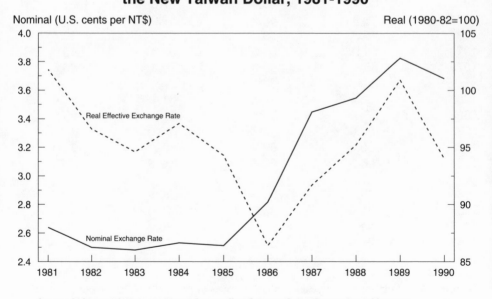

Sources: GAO report NSIAD-89-130; Morgan Guaranty Trust Company; Federal Reserve Board of Governors.

of the Korean won. By 1989, the Taiwanese real exchange rate was above its 1982–84 average, while the Korean rate was still lower than its 1982–84 level. Thus Taiwan has made more of an effort than Korea to use exchange rate adjustment to offset its rising competitiveness and thus to restrain its trade surpluses. This difference in the use of exchange rate adjustment is reflected in the data in Table 13, which show that Taiwan's unit labor costs rose much more on a U.S. dollar basis than on a national currency basis from 1986 to 1989. Taiwan's exchange rate policies thus worked to offset its competitive advantages in unit labor costs, rather than to reinforce them, although some of this progress seems to have been reversed in 1990.

The Taiwanese example provides another instance in which structural barriers to trade have a macroeconomic impact on the trade balance.

In spite of the appreciation of the Taiwan dollar, both Taiwan's overall trade surplus and its bilateral surplus with the U.S. grew rapidly until 1987, and have remained large since then. In 1990, the U.S. merchandise trade deficit with Taiwan was $11.2 billion—down considerably from the 1987 peak deficit of $17.2 billion, but still representing 11 percent of the total U.S. deficit for merchandise trade (on a customs basis) for 1990. What accounts for this persistent large trade imbalance, in spite of Taiwan's efforts to adjust its exchange rate?

Moreno (1989) found that Taiwan has an unusually low income elasticity of demand for imports (0.82). This low income elasticity combined with relatively slow growth of domestic demand accounts for most of the rise in Taiwan's trade surplus, according to Moreno's econometric estimates. While the appreciation of the Taiwan dollar kept the surpluses from being even larger, Taiwan nevertheless relied on a conflictive form of export-led growth, exporting unemployment to deficit countries such as the United States.

The Taiwanese example provides another instance in which structural barriers to trade have a macroeconomic impact on the trade balance. The low income elasticity of import demand in Taiwan reflects the strong barriers, both formal and informal, to imports—especially of consumer goods, but also of producer goods for which the government wants to encourage domestic production (see Smith, 1991). These barriers have thus contributed very directly to sustaining Taiwan's trade surpluses, in spite of exchange rate policies which, by themselves, would have tended to reduce those surpluses. Once again, we find that structural reforms—in this case, market-opening measures in

Taiwan—could help to reduce a country's trade surplus. The extent to which the U.S. would benefit from this would then depend on the competitiveness of U.S. versus Japanese and European products.

The Latin American Debtors

The sudden withdrawal of foreign lending had a devastating impact on nations whose economic growth had been largely dependent on external finance.

Like the East Asian NICs, the more industrially advanced countries of Latin America (especially Mexico and Brazil) can achieve substantial labor cost advantages over the United States by combining capital-intensive methods and modern technology with low wages. Of course, in strictly labor-intensive activities, even some of the poorest Latin nations (e.g., the Dominican Republic) enjoy advantages in unit labor costs. But Brazil and Mexico can also export relatively complex, capital-intensive products (e.g., steel, auto parts, and even small airplanes). As in East Asia, these competitive advantages alone do not dictate trade surpluses; macroeconomic conditions and policies must also be taken into account.

The dominant macroeconomic phenomenon in Latin America in the 1980s was the burden of adjustment to the debt crisis (see Dornbusch, 1985; Sachs, ed., 1989; and Taylor, 1988). When the debtor nations became unable to service their debts, creditor nations and private banks cut off further lending. The sudden withdrawal of foreign lending had a devastating impact on nations whose economic growth had been largely dependent on external finance. The growth of Mexican GDP per capita fell from an average annual rate of 3.4 percent in 1965–1980 to – 1.7 percent in 1980–88; Brazilian growth fell by the same measure from 6.4 percent in 1965–1980 to 0.7 percent in 1980–88.[6] In Latin America and the Caribbean as a whole, per capita GDP growth fell from an average annual rate of 3.5 percent in 1965–1980 to – 0.7 percent in 1980–88. Domestic investment was especially hard hit: total Latin American gross investment spending *fell* at an average annual rate of 2.1 percent from 1981–88, after rising at an average rate of 7.3 percent per year from 1961–1980 (Inter-American Development Bank, 1989, p. 11). Throughout the region, real wages fell sharply, poverty increased dramatically, and two decades of development progress were reversed in just a few short years.[7]

The depression of Latin American growth affected its external balance in several interrelated ways. First, demand for imports fell off as there was neither domestic income nor foreign exchange to pay for them. In Latin America as a whole, import demand *fell* by 2.5 percent per year from 1981–88, after rising by 5.7 percent per year from 1961–70 and 8.1 percent per year from 1971–80 (Inter-American Development Bank, 1989, p. 11). Since a large portion of Latin American investment spending went to purchase imported capital goods, the effect was especially devastating on capital goods exporters in the industrialized nations (especially the United States). In addition, large amounts of domestic savings (including, perversely, funds borrowed from abroad) were sent out of Latin America in what was called "capital flight" (see Lessard and Williamson, 1987; Pastor, 1989). Capital flight only exacerbated the problems of servicing external debts and financing both imports and domestic investment.

In the early 1980s, U.S. exports to Mexico and Brazil collapsed.

Second, since foreign exchange was required both to service the debt (where and when it was serviced) and to pay for needed imports, and since sources of external borrowing had dried up, Latin American nations had to promote exports as rapidly as possible (see Frischtak, 1989, on the Brazilian case). These export promotion efforts were aided by the currency devaluations and real wage cuts adopted as part of the economic "stabilization" policy packages promoted by the International Monetary Fund and the U.S. government. Where efforts at restraining imports and promoting exports succeeded, Latin American nations swung from trade deficits to surpluses—in effect, becoming net exporters of resources to the much richer creditor nations.

How these changes affected the U.S. trade balance may be seen from Figures 22 and 23, which depict U.S. merchandise trade with Mexico and Brazil (respectively) from 1970 to 1990. These two figures are drawn with logarithmic scales in order to smooth out the effects of inflation and to emphasize the proportional differences between exports and imports (rather than the absolute dollar differences). The U.S. had trade surpluses with these two countries in the 1970s, financed by net foreign investment (including the loans which led to the debt crisis). Then, in the early 1980s, U.S. exports to Mexico and Brazil collapsed as those countries' macroeconomic crises erupted. U.S. imports from Mexico and Brazil did not increase unusually rapidly in the 1980s, but continued to grow (in current dollars) at more or less the same rate as in the 1970s (especially if one discounts the oil-led surge in imports from Mexico in 1978–1980). Thus it was mainly the collapse of Latin

Figure 22

U.S. Merchandise Trade With Mexico, 1970-1990

Millions of U.S. Dollars (Logarithmic Scale)

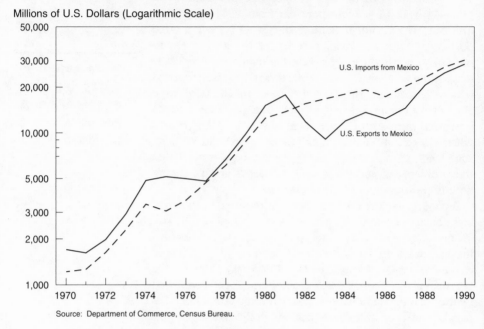

Source: Department of Commerce, Census Bureau.

Figure 23
U.S. Merchandise Trade With Brazil, 1970-1990

Millions of U.S. Dollars (Logarithmic Scale)

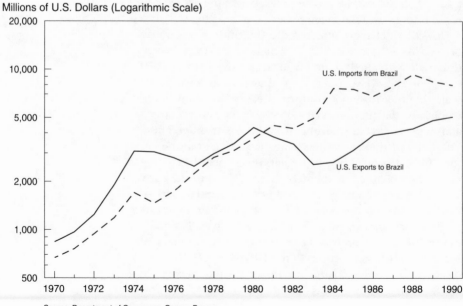

Source: Department of Commerce, Census Bureau.

American growth, rather than successful export promotion efforts, which led to chronic U.S. trade deficits with this region in the 1980s.

U.S. exports to Mexico picked up in 1988–1990, resulting in a much narrower trade gap. This rise in U.S. exports is largely a result of the remarkable opening of the Mexican market to imports, especially of consumer goods, as a result of President de la Madrid's 1987 decision (under U.S. and IMF pressure) to liberalize Mexican trade.[8] But this is likely to be a once-and-for all step up in Mexican imports from the U.S.

Indeed, Mexico's interest in a free trade agreement with the U.S. under the Salinas administration can be attributed in part to a desire to balance out Mexico's one-sided liberalization of imports with greater access to the U.S. market. Such an agreement could improve the U.S. trade balance in the short run, as increased direct foreign investment by U.S. firms in Mexico would result in some recovery of capital goods exports from the U.S. (although Japanese and other foreign firms would also benefit). But in the long run, Mexico would become an enormous platform for low-wage exports back to the U.S., and the bilateral trade balance would probably shift back in favor of Mexico.

It was mainly the collapse of Latin American growth, rather than successful export promotion efforts, which led to chronic U.S. trade deficits with this region.

Endnotes

1   The Mexican peso was overvalued at that time. It was devalued from a fixed rate of 12.50 pesos per dollar in 1975 to about 22 per dollar in 1976. The peso was also somewhat overvalued in 1980 due to the Mexican oil boom.

2   Even this lower figure for Mexico is exaggerated, since this measure of Mexican manufacturing compensation does not include the export-oriented maquiladoras where wages are about half those in national industries on average.

3   This has been acknowledged by at least one leading international economist, Rudiger Dornbusch (1989a, p. 111), who said: "[An] argument that used to be advanced is that low wages in the NICs reflect low levels of productivity. That . . . is now understood to be wrong in many cases. Productivity levels in many industries are at the U.S. levels, but wages are only one-tenth our level."

4   In this model, marginal labor productivity is assumed to be constant and is therefore equal to average productivity in each industry. The average for the whole economy would be weighted by trade shares consistent with balanced trade. For a theoretical treatment of this model see Dornbusch, Fischer, and Samuelson (1977).

5   Based on data in International Monetary Fund, *International Financial Statistics*, August 1990. Taiwan's reserves of foreign exchange excluding gold were worth SDR55.719 billion at the end of 1989, while the SDR was valued at US$1.31416.

6   Growth rates for GDP per capita are calculated from data in World Bank, *World Development Report 1990*, Tables 2 and 26.

7   See Dornbusch (1988b) and Lustig (1990a) for detailed studies of the Mexican case.

8   See Cypher (1990) on the political economy of Mexico's economic liberalization policies.

114

Chapter 7

Implications for Policy

The central message of this report is that the U.S. trade deficit does not result from macro policy mistakes alone. Structural problems, including closed markets and low unit labor costs abroad, along with declining competitiveness and the loss of technological leadership at home, have contributed substantially to the worsening of the U.S. trade position. These problems not only have had independent effects on the U.S. trade balance, but also have exacerbated the effects of macro policies (both domestic and foreign, fiscal and monetary) on trade. Moreover, the existence of such structural problems implies that efforts to restore balanced trade with macro policy corrections (e.g., budget deficit reduction and dollar depreciation) alone are likely to have severely depressing effects on domestic employment, incomes, and living standards.

It is often said that in order to cure the trade deficit, the United States needs to get its own house in order first. If this proposition is interpreted narrowly as implying that all we need to do is to cut the federal budget deficit and squeeze private consumption in order to raise the national saving rate, then it is at best a beggar-ourselves solution. Nevertheless, this proposition contains a germ of truth, if it is interpreted more broadly. The U.S. needs to adopt a new perspective on economic policymaking which puts a priority on fostering competitiveness in domestic industries. While macro policies can and must support this effort, they must also be accompanied by micro-level industrial policies designed to promote the commercial application of technological innovations, the modernization of

The U.S. needs to adopt a new perspective on economic policymaking which puts a priority on fostering competitiveness in domestic industries.

import-competing sectors, and investment in high value-added activities offering high-wage employment.

Trade policies designed to influence U.S. relations with other countries cannot substitute for such reforms of domestic policy. Nevertheless, trade policies can be used to counteract the effects of (or to induce changes in) foreign institutions or practices which have a negative impact on the U.S. trade position. Properly designed trade policies can play a positive role in resolving global imbalances without placing too much of the burden of adjustment on American taxpayers and consumers. Based on the analysis in this report, the trade policy responses need to be tailored to address the particular problems in the bilateral trade relations between the U.S. and those nations with which we have had large and persistent trade deficits, especially Japan and the East Asian NICs, and to a lesser extent Germany and the Latin American debtors. In this concluding chapter, I will sketch the broad outlines of an appropriate package of effective trade remedies. I will also evaluate the role that macroeconomic policy can and should play in fostering a high-income, growth-oriented solution to the trade deficit problem.

> *Trade policy responses need to be tailored to address the particular problems in the bilateral trade relations between the U.S. and those nations with which we have had large and persistent trade deficits.*

Policies for Industrial Surplus Countries

With regard to the other industrialized nations, especially Japan and Germany, the first priority must be placed on efforts to keep the United States at the frontier of technological progress in the leading sectors with the greatest growth prospects. It is neither necessary nor feasible to ensure a U.S. monopoly of technological leadership in all areas. But it is essential at least to stay in the game in a broad spectrum of high-tech sectors, and to try to maintain leadership in some. It would be beyond the scope of this report to evaluate which specific kinds of measures (in areas such as education, R&D, infrastructure, antitrust, etc.) would be most effective in this regard, and exactly what role the government should play in the process. The point to be emphasized here is that if effective measures to promote technological competitiveness are implemented, they *can* have a positive impact both on the trade balance for any given set of macroeconomic conditions—or in relieving the macroeconomic costs of achieving balanced trade. It is also important to stress that the key objective should be the *location* of technologically advanced production in the U.S., not simply the national ownership of the corporations engaged in such production regardless of where the production is located (see Reich, 1990).

A second but related priority is to confront the challenges posed by foreign policies and institutions which affect industrial development and international trade—whether those policies and institutions are explicitly trade-oriented or not. The Japanese case clearly presents the greatest such challenge. On the one hand, Japan has had an industrial development strategy which rests on export promotion; on the other hand, Japan's institutions effectively keep its market relatively closed to manufactured imports. This combination makes it difficult for other countries to maintain balanced trade while still achieving their own growth objectives. It is not surprising, therefore, that Japan has had the largest and most persistent bilateral trade surplus with the U.S.—and that this surplus arose in a decade when U.S. growth recovered relative to Japan's.[1]

In the case of Japan, then, it seems reasonable to use trade policy as a lever for inducing desired changes in Japan's own trade practices, or—if that is not possible—then at least to offset their effects on the United States. As advocated by Dornbusch (1990) and Salvatore (1990), one appropriate tool is some kind of import surcharge levied on Japanese imports into the U.S., to be suspended if Japan meets specified targets for increasing its imports of U.S. manufactures. This is a reasonable and appropriate counterweight to the institutions and practices which keep Japan's share of manufactured imports so low. It allows the Japanese themselves to decide how to reform their system so as to encourage more imports of manufactures, but it does not allow them to rely on imports of primary products for reducing their trade surplus. And unlike so-called "voluntary restraint agreements" (VRAs), an import surcharge (if actually levied) would yield extra revenue for the U.S. government rather than excess profits for Japanese exporters.[2]

The German case does not seem to require special trade policies. Although West Germany's postwar growth was largely export-led, the German market has been much more open than the Japanese. Moreover, as a result of Western European integration in EC 1992 along with the opening up of Eastern Europe and the former Soviet Union to foreign trade and investment, it is likely that German trade will be more oriented to other parts of Europe in the future. The process of reconstructing the economy of the former East Germany will further distract German eco-

One appropriate tool is some kind of import surcharge levied on Japanese imports into the U.S., to be suspended if Japan meets specified targets for increasing its imports of U.S. manufactures.

nomic efforts in the 1990s. And, as we have seen, the German bilateral surplus with the U.S. has basically risen and fallen with the DM/$ exchange rate. Unfortunately, the dollar has been appreciating against the DM recently (in early 1991), rising back to over 1.70DM per dollar, after trading at under 1.50DM per dollar in late 1990. It would be appropriate to target a lower value for the deutschemark and to use monetary policies and exchange market intervention to keep the actual exchange rate close to the target.

In the future, the relevant competitor for the U.S. may be the EC as a whole rather than Germany alone. In one respect, this is reassuring, since the U.S. now has a trade surplus with the EC as a whole (although it is much smaller than in the past). However, the prospect of a more inward-oriented Europe will pose some challenges for U.S. trade policy. One particularly important area is domestic content legislation. Many European countries require multinational firms investing in them to achieve targeted percentages of local production and sourcing. This puts the U.S. at a disadvantage insofar as we have no parallel regulations, which leaves both national and foreign firms operating here free to maximize imports of parts and components. A negotiated harmonization of local content regulation between the EC and the U.S. could help to ensure that the former does not unduly restrict its imports to the detriment of producers located in the latter. Adopting domestic content measures in the U.S. (together with Canada) could help to assure a balanced distribution of global manufacturing production between this country and other industrialized nations.

Another area in which harmonization with the EC is needed is subsidies. The United States has generally been unsuccessful in convincing the EC to abandon its industrial as well as its agricultural subsidies. An alternative approach would be for the U.S. to drop its ideological opposition to subsidizing domestic production in vital industries. Then we could negotiate pragmatic rules allowing subsidies in industries where it makes sense—especially in high-tech sectors promising "external" economies or social benefits not captured in market prices or private returns. On the other hand, subsidies which merely create excess capacity in mature industries could be phased out gradually so as to permit such industries in all nations to shrink proportionally over some reasonable time frame, with adequate provision for worker retraining and other adjustment costs.

The prospect of a more inward-oriented Europe will pose some challenges for U.S. trade policy.

118

Policies for Developing Surplus Countries

Turning to the NICs, we have seen that the main trade problem with these countries stems from their ability to sustain across-the-board advantages in manufacturing unit labor costs by combining low wages with relatively high productivity through technology transfers and direct foreign investment. The most successful NICs, especially Taiwan and Korea, have taken advantage of low unit labor costs and undervalued currencies to sustain large trade surpluses while amassing large foreign currency reserves. Like Germany and Japan before them, they are following the classic beggar-thy-neighbor policy of exporting unemployment to those countries (especially the U.S.) which freely accept their manufactured imports.

Economic theory suggests a simple and direct remedy for offsetting these nations' competitive advantages in labor costs: revaluation (appreciation) of their currencies. The problem has been that, in practice, there does not exist any automatic mechanism to compel such a revaluation. The NICs have managed exchange rate regimes, preventing the U.S. from intervening in foreign exchange markets to make the dollar fall against their currencies, as the U.S. can against the Japanese yen and European currencies which are freely traded in global financial markets. It would take conscious policy decisions on the part of the NIC governments to revalue their currencies to levels that would offset their absolute advantages in manufacturing unit labor costs. The NICs benefit from the asymmetry which has always plagued any system of fixed exchange rates: the surplus countries are not forced to adjust, as long as they can "sterilize" the accumulation of foreign exchange reserves so as to prevent inflationary effects.[3]

Up to now, the U.S. has tried to use its political leverage combined with implicit threats of greater protectionism to induce the NICs to revalue. As discussed in Chapter 6, the results have been mixed, with greater success in the case of Taiwan than Korea, and with some backsliding in both nations in the last year. In order to ensure further progress toward revaluation of their currencies, the U.S. should impose a "unit labor cost equalization surcharge"[4] on imports of manufactures from NICs with chronic trade surpluses, subject to certain conditions to be spelled out below. The affected countries could avoid the surcharge by allowing their currencies to appreciate (or their wages to

Economic theory suggests a simple and direct remedy for offsetting these nations' competitive advantages in labor costs: revaluation . . . of their currencies.

119

increase) to a level which would keep their average manufacturing unit labor costs (in dollars) within a reasonable range of the U.S. average, as determined by the Bureau of Labor Statistics (BLS) in the U.S. Department of Labor. If it is too difficult to compare NIC unit labor costs with U.S. costs in absolute terms, then targets could be set for *increases* in NIC unit labor costs in dollars (which the BLS already measures, as shown in Table 13 above).

The U.S. should impose a "unit labor cost equalization surcharge" on imports of manufactures from NICs with chronic trade surpluses.

Leaving aside wage increases for the moment, it is clear that the NICs would have strong incentives to choose the option of currency appreciation over accepting the surcharge. Both options make their exports less competitive in price terms, but appreciation improves their "terms of trade" (i.e., increases their purchasing power over imports) while the surcharge does not. If they realize that they have no choice but to accept reduced price competitiveness, then they should surely prefer the alternative which at least offers such compensation. This requires a credible threat that a surcharge will actually be imposed (say, through some automatic mechanism) if they fail to raise their average unit labor costs in dollars sufficiently.

Some restrictions should be placed on the threat of an import surcharge in order to prevent inequitable outcomes. Such a threat should only be made in the cases of NICs which meet the following criteria: (1) chronic trade surpluses; and (2) overvalued currencies, as indicated by *both* (a) low unit labor costs in dollars *and* (b) evidence of substantial foreign exchange market intervention to prevent currency appreciation (e.g., a large accumulation of international reserves). Thus, the policy proposed here is *not* intended for application to all "low-wage" countries. Indeed, the most impoverished and lowest-wage LDCs (most of Africa and southern Asia) would be exempted, since they are unlikely to meet criteria (1) and (2b) even if they meet (2a). There is no point in penalizing the poorest nations on earth in order to help one of the richest countries balance its trade. But some new export powerhouses which meet these criteria (e.g., China) could be subject to the surcharge.

While currency appreciation is important for eliminating Korea and Taiwan's absolute advantages in unit labor costs, it will not be sufficient for eliminating these countries' trade surpluses unless accompanied by market-opening reforms and more expansionary domestic demand policies (Moreno, 1989). As discussed earlier, these countries have

120

followed the Japanese model by deliberately restraining domestic demand and relying on external markets to stimulate growth, while keeping import markets closed through all kinds of formal and informal barriers (Amsden, 1979 and 1989; Smith, 1991). Liberalization of import barriers is especially important for the revaluation of their currencies to translate into lower prices of imported goods (and of domestic products which compete with imports) at home.

An important aspect of the export-led growth strategy in the NICs has been to keep real wage gains lagging behind productivity gains. While on the one hand this keeps their unit labor costs low (at least in domestic currency terms), on the other hand it serves to inhibit the expansion of their internal markets by suppressing the growth of workers' consumption. Currency appreciation and import liberalization can help to raise real wages for Korean and Taiwanese workers by making consumption goods cheaper, but more direct efforts to raise wages may also be appropriate.

In order for workers to be able to win greater wage increases in the NICs, it is important to remedy the gross violations of basic worker rights (e.g., unionization, minimum wages, health and safety standards) that are found in many of these countries (along with poorer LDCs). These violations sometimes extend to physical violence against workers who protest or organize. Apart from their evident moral repugnance, such violations of labor rights reduce workers' bargaining leverage, and thus restrict their ability to obtain fair remuneration for their (increasingly productive) labor.

At present, most advocates of international labor rights in the United States have focused on trying to reform U.S. trade laws to include labor rights provisions. While there have been some small legislative successes, discretionary enforcement under the Reagan and Bush administrations has rendered the existing labor rights provisions ineffective except as a political tool against disfavored regimes.[5]

Unfortunately, the U.S. is in a poor position to promote labor rights in other nations today, given the weakening of labor rights at home and our habit of selective enforcement of existing human and labor rights laws based on political criteria. Getting labor rights provisions into international trade agreements such as the General Agreement on Trade and Tariffs (GATT) would be more desirable than trying to enforce them unilaterally through U.S. law, but we are very far from even getting such provisions introduced. It is hard

Currency appreciation will not be sufficient for eliminating these countries' trade surpluses unless accompanied by market-opening reforms and more expansionary domestic demand policies.

enough to achieve effective labor rights in one's own country; it is much harder to enforce such rights on other nations with different histories and institutions.

The strategy advocated here—a surcharge to countervail against low unit labor costs, used as a device to induce currency revaluation—is much easier to enact and to enforce than labor rights measures, because it can be done through the ordinary instruments of trade policy (tariffs and exchange rates), without any need to intervene in (or sit in judgment of) other countries' internal institutions and politics. If in fact the NICs respond by revaluing their currencies (and also by opening up their own markets), the effect should be to lower the cost of living and thus to raise real wages for their workers. Moreover, such a strategy would weaken the incentives for employers in the NICs to violate labor rights in order to suppress wages, since wage suppression would be offset by a countervailing surcharge. While this would not cure all labor rights violations—especially those which relate to working conditions—it could at least help to tilt the scales in wage bargaining more in favor of workers in the NICs.

If in fact the NICs respond by revaluing their currencies (and also by opening up their own markets), the effect should be to . . . raise real wages for their workers.

In the cases of the East Asian NICs, their wages have already risen considerably relative to U.S. wages in dollar terms, as shown in Table 12 above. Most of this improvement is due to the late 1980s appreciation of their currencies shown in Figures 20 and 21 for Korea and Taiwan (see also Table 13 on the trends in Korean and Taiwanese unit labor costs in dollars)—although the competitive pressure of low-wage imports has undoubtedly also contributed to slow wage growth in the United States. Further currency appreciation combined with trade liberalization in the NICs could help raise their domestic real wages further by making consumption goods cheaper (whether those goods are directly imported, produced with imported inputs, or merely competitive with imports). And a redistribution of income to wages would help to encourage the expansion of domestic demand in the NICs, which would also aid in reducing their trade surpluses.

For these reasons, the policy advocated here is potentially beneficial to workers in the NICs. While their employment growth may slacken in the short run, employed workers should enjoy higher real wages—more of the fruits of their highly productive labor—than they currently receive. The objective of compelling the NICs to revalue their currencies is thus not to block their development, but rather to induce them to take more of the benefits of their development in the form of higher domestic wages and living standards. In the long run, they should be able to sustain high employment through domestic demand-led growth rather than export-led growth which relies on low wages and imbalanced trade.

Policies for Developing Debtor Countries

The heavily indebted Latin American NICs, such as Mexico and Brazil, should be exempted from the unit labor cost equalization policy proposed above. While they do of course have low unit labor costs in dollars, their lack of large accumulations of international reserves—itself a symptom of their financial crises—indicates that they have not been keeping their currencies artificially undervalued. On the contrary, it is generally thought that these countries have tended to have overvalued currencies in the past (World Bank, 1987), and that their recent devaluations have been necessary to restore their international competitiveness. To punish them further for their painful stabilization efforts would be perverse.

As shown in Table 12 (above), wages in the Latin American debtor nations collapsed while wages in the East Asian NICs were rising in the 1980s. The collapse in Latin American wages is largely attributable to the macroeconomic repercussions of the debt crisis, including the need for currency depreciation as well as drastic cuts in social spending and low or negative rates of economic growth. There can be no recuperation of Latin American wages until the macroeconomic disorder in these countries—whether due to domestic mismanagement or external constraints or both—is remedied. Unless and until the burden of servicing their crushing debts is alleviated, and new sources of capital inflows become available, these countries will be unable to resume rapid economic growth. And until they can resume rapid growth, their demand for U.S. exports will remain depressed, relative to past trends.

From the standpoint of U.S. policy, the most important thing that can be done to aid Latin America is greater debt relief combined with other efforts to reverse the net outflow of resources from Latin America. The simplest way to extend debt relief is to forgive a substantial part of the principal on outstanding loans, as was recently done for Poland. Another way would be to limit debt service to a fixed percentage of export earnings until the debtor economies have

Wages in the Latin American debtor nations collapsed while wages in the East Asian NICs were rising in the 1980s.

recovered. Many other proposals have been advanced to refinance the debts by having some international agency buy them up at a discount (say, at their secondary market value) and then allow the debtor nations to pay back the discounted loans on favorable terms. The specifics of such proposals need not concern us here.

What is important to emphasize for present purposes is that greater debt relief can be a win-win exchange for both the U.S. and Latin American economies. While the gains for Latin America may be obvious, the gains for the United States are no less significant. On the one hand, the Latin American countries could afford to grow faster and to import more U.S. products. On the other hand, there would be less pressure on Latin American countries to push exports in order to garner excess foreign exchange earnings for debt service. For both reasons, the U.S. trade balance with Latin America would be improved. And since U.S. banks have greatly reduced their exposure to Latin American loans, and have already set aside considerable reserves to cover losses on those loans, the danger to the U.S. banking system from greater debt relief is now relatively small (although U.S. banks are now in trouble mainly for other reasons).[6]

> **Greater debt relief can be a win-win exchange for both the U.S. and Latin American economies.**

It is also essential to channel new net capital inflows into Latin America in order to revive its economic growth.[7] Given the bad experiences of the late 1970s and early 1980s, this should *not* be done through private commercial bank lending. What is needed is a Marshall Plan for recovering debtor nations, with funds contributed by the surplus countries (not only Japan and Germany, but also surplus NICs like Korea and Taiwan and oil exporters like Saudi Arabia) and channeled through a multilateral agency such as the World Bank. Such a redirection of global surpluses from investment in U.S. financial assets to investment in Third World development would help to revive global growth, restore equity in the debtor countries, and reduce the burden of international trade imbalances.

Unfortunately, the Bush administration is moving in a very different direction in its economic policies toward Latin America—a direction which puts the interests of U.S. banks and corporations ahead of the interests of U.S. workers. The Bush administration is pushing for a free trade agreement with Mexico, which would expand the U.S.-Canada free trade area (FTA) into a North American FTA. Beyond this, the administration is promoting an

"Enterprise for the Americas" initiative which would try to induce other Latin American nations to join in a hemispheric FTA. With this new initiative, the Bush administration is forgetting even its own miserly program for debt relief, the Brady Plan, which offered minimal debt relief with heavy conditionality in regard to domestic economic policies.[8]

Although the proposals for expanded free trade with Latin America are not explicitly presented as alternatives to debt relief, it is clear in fact that the former are intended partly as substitutes for the latter. The FTA proposals aim to get foreign capital into Latin America (starting with Mexico) mainly via a different channel—direct investment by multinational corporations in production of goods for export back to the U.S. market.

The proposals for expanded free trade with Latin America are . . . intended partly as substitutes for [debt relief].

Indeed, a greater opening to direct investment by U.S. multinationals in Mexico has to be seen as the main economic objective of the Bush administration in an FTA with Mexico. Mexico has already liberalized its import restrictions considerably in the last few years, except in a few sectors such as automobiles. There is thus relatively little room left for tariff reductions or other pure trade liberalization measures on the Mexican side of the border. However, opening up the U.S. market more to Mexican exports, combined with further relaxation of Mexican restrictions on direct foreign investment, would encourage more U.S. firms (as well as Japanese and others) to relocate production in a country where manufacturing wages average only 16 percent of the U.S. level (even less in the maquiladora export assembly plants), and where labor standards and environmental regulations are poorly enforced.

Advocates of the U.S.-Mexico FTA (e.g., Dornbusch, Krugman, and Park, 1989) advertise that it will increase exports of capital equipment; they fail to advertise that the exported capital equipment will soon be used to generate imports that will replace U.S. products in one industry after another. In the most hopeful scenario, a U.S.-Mexico FTA will stimulate so much foreign investment south of the border that Mexican growth will revive, perhaps enough to give the U.S. a trade surplus with its neighbor (U.S. International Trade Commission, 1991). While it is not explicitly stated, such investment would then allow Mexico to continue servicing its outstanding debts without the need for any further relief beyond that already granted under the Brady Plan. Mexico would get more manufacturing jobs, but only as long as it maintained its "advantage" in low wages and environmental decay. As one Mexican critic has written,

> What we are witnessing is [not a coequal integration but] rather the assimilation of certain segments of the Mexican economy into the [U.S. economy]; which represents, for Mexico, a process of national disintegration and for the United States a selective and discriminatory exploitation of certain advantages which the Mexican economy offers. (Aguilar Zinser, 1989–1990, p. 66, translated by this author)

While this process will undoubtedly be profitable for U.S. corporations, and may even bring short-run trade benefits, the long run impact will only be to speed up the transfer of manufacturing activities to lower-wage regions which underlies much of the structural declining trend in U.S. competitiveness. U.S. industry and employment would continue to be sacrificed to the interests of the large banks and multinational corporations.

One largely unexploited area of possible U.S. trade advantages is Eastern Europe and the former U.S.S.R.

Other Countries

One largely unexploited area of possible U.S. trade advantages is Eastern Europe and the former U.S.S.R. The U.S. has long had trade surpluses with the ex-Soviet Bloc countries, although those surpluses have diminished somewhat in recent years (see Tables 6 and 7, above). But with those countries reforming their internal structures and opening up more to foreign trade, the prospects for U.S. export growth are potentially very great. The reason is, quite simply, that the U.S. offers exactly what Eastern European countries and the ex-Soviet republics need, especially capital equipment of all kinds (for construction, manufacturing, pollution control, etc.) as well as food products. One recent study projected that total U.S. trade (exports plus imports) with the Soviet Union alone could swell to $94.7 billion by 2010, from a mere $3.4 billion in 1988 (Feinberg, Echeverri-Gent, and Müller, 1990, p. 235).

The main problem in promoting such trade (assuming the continuation of economic reform in Eastern Europe and the ex-U.S.S.R.) is financing it. Those countries need massive injections of foreign capital in order to finance their imports from the West before they become competitive enough to earn their foreign exchange through exports. As in the case of Latin America, it is necessary to arrange a

126

global program for mobilizing current account surpluses to be invested in Eastern Europe and the former Soviet republics, in order to finance the increased imports they will require during their transition to market-based economies. Policies aimed at mobilizing such resources could have an enormous payoff for the United States by opening up vast new foreign markets—provided that our industries are poised to supply the goods which Eastern Europe and the ex-U.S.S.R. will demand.

A Note on Energy Policy

Although it has not been a major focus of this report, energy policy is clearly important for improving the U.S. trade position. U.S. petroleum imports totalled $62.3 billion in 1990, representing nearly 60 percent of the year's merchandise trade deficit on a national income account basis. And the Persian Gulf crisis in 1990–91 served as a reminder of continued U.S. vulnerability to oil price shocks due to foreign events. In spite of these persistent problems, the U.S. has no coherent policy in place for reducing its energy consumption and dependency on imported oil in the long run. The Bush administration's proposed energy strategy essentially amounts to giving energy producers a free hand to exploit precious natural resources in order to satisfy our currently high level of energy consumption, rather than to try to reduce that level over time.

As discussed earlier (in Chapter 4), U.S. economic growth historically depended on abundant and cheap domestic energy resources. Since the basis for this energy-intensive form of economic growth has eroded, the nation needs to make adjustments in order to conserve its increasingly scarce and expensive domestic energy resources. In addition, the country needs to seek ways of insulating itself as much as possible from foreign energy supply shocks. A comprehensive energy policy to deal with these problems would have to encompass a number of coordinated elements. First, it is appropriate to let the price of energy rise in real terms in the long run—but also to phase in price increases gradually. And second, we need to reemphasize mandated conservation measures such as increasing fuel economies along with improved public transportation alternatives to the automobile.

Energy taxes can be an important part of an overall energy strategy. Such taxes should be raised slowly in order to minimize the impact on highly energy-dependent con-

> **Energy policy is clearly important for improving the U.S. trade position.**

sumers and producers. Energy taxes should not be set at rigid rates, however, but should be flexible in response to changes in world energy prices so as to maintain a steady upward trend in domestic energy prices. Predictability of gradually rising energy prices is vital for enabling producers and consumers to plan the adoption of energy-saving technologies and other conservation measures.

Energy taxes could include either an oil import surcharge or a domestic energy consumption levy, each of which has its advantages and disadvantages. An import surcharge would reduce demand for imported oil and, since the U.S. is a large consumer of oil on the world market, could help to hold down the world price of oil by counteracting the monopoly power of the Organization of Petroleum Exporting Countries (OPEC). An import surcharge could also be adjusted relatively easily in order to offset international price shocks. However, an oil import surcharge by itself would encourage more domestic production, which is not necessarily desirable. Greater domestic production would encourage the more rapid depletion of U.S. petroleum and other energy reserves, as well as threaten vulnerable parts of the environment (e.g., through offshore drilling).

For these reasons, a domestic energy consumption tax would be preferable. Such taxes already exist, of course, but there is much room for rationalizing the myriad state excise taxes on a national basis and phasing in a rate structure based on long-term conservation objectives rather than short-term revenue needs. Also, energy tax revenues should be targeted more for financing conservation measures (including the improvement of mass transit alternatives), not just for encouraging more highway construction. One strategy would be to use a domestic energy consumption tax to induce (and fund) conservation, while complementing it with a flexible oil import surcharge used primarily as a price-stabilizing device.

But energy taxes, however implemented, should not be the only means of discouraging energy-intensive production methods and consumption patterns. By themselves, such taxes can introduce great inequities for people who have no alternatives to using their energy-inefficient cars or other consumer durables. This includes middle-class rural and suburban dwellers, who live in areas designed for total dependency on the automobile, as well as low-income consumers with no affordable alternatives for heating their

Energy tax revenues should be targeted more for financing conservation measures.

homes or driving to work. While suitable income tax rebates for energy taxes could partly alleviate such inequities, it would be difficult to eliminate all the inequities this way.

These considerations of equity as well as the environmental interest in conservation argue for supplementing energy taxes with more direct measures for increasing national energy efficiency. This should include both expanded mass transit facilities where feasible, and new zoning laws to make newer communities better designed for mass transit. High speed trains could replace airplanes for short and medium distance travel, while leaving the airlines to cover long distance routes. Loans and subsidies for developing alternative energy sources (e.g., solar) should be reintroduced, along with programs to help low- and middle-income families and small businesses purchase more energy-efficient equipment. These types of measures would have important side benefits for clean air as well as for preserving national parks and coastlines from excessive exploitation for energy extraction.

Every dollar of reduced spending on oil imports lessens the degree of other adjustments and sacrifices which are required to achieve balanced trade.

But the bottom line, for present purposes, is that every dollar of reduced spending on oil imports lessens the degree of other adjustments and sacrifices which are required to achieve balanced trade. Energy conservation is another type of structural reform that can help to alleviate the macroeconomic costs of eliminating the trade deficit. And it is vital to combine tax policies which work through the price system with more direct conservation measures in order to construct a coherent and equitable energy policy.

Macroeconomic and Exchange Rate Policies

Although macroeconomic policies alone cannot solve the U.S. trade deficit at an acceptable social cost, this does not mean that macro policies have no role to play. Growing budget deficits at home, coupled with contractionary fiscal policies abroad, did contribute to some extent to the rise in the U.S. trade deficit in the 1980s. And tight monetary policies that raised real interest rates did spark the overvaluation of the dollar in the early 1980s. A coherent package for addressing the trade imbalance must include fiscal and monetary policy changes which would help keep U.S. products competitive and improve the trade balance without undue domestic austerity or sacrifices of living standards.

The goal of fiscal policy adjustment should not be a balanced budget, even at full employment, especially since the federal budget includes capital expenditures that no private company or household would insist on financing out of current revenue. Nor does it make sense to rely on cutting the fiscal deficit as the primary tool for reducing the trade deficit. Since every $1 of fiscal cuts yields no more than 30¢ of current account improvement, it would take at least $300 billion of budget deficit reductions to eliminate the current account deficit (which was roughly $90 billion in 1990), holding other factors constant. Such a massive fiscal contraction would produce a severe economic depression, and is not politically feasible anyway.

Rather, fiscal policy should be targeted at some sensible long-run domestic goal. One reasonable goal would be to stabilize the national debt as a percentage of GNP. This would keep the government interest burden from increasing proportionately to national output, especially if combined with monetary policies fostering lower interest rates. Alternatively, we could seek to limit the high-employment budget deficit to the amount of public investment spending, so that only currently operating expenditures, including debt service, would have to be financed out of current revenue when the economy is not in a recession. Either of these goals could be achieved in the 1990s with modest rather than draconian fiscal adjustments.[9]

As the economy recovers from the 1990–91 recession, gradual measures to reduce the federal budget deficit along these lines could be implemented. These measures should focus first on restoring the progressivity of the tax system. Such a focus is justified not only by considerations of fairness and equity, but also by macroeconomic objectives. As argued earlier (in Chapter 2), the reduced effective taxation of income from capital has been responsible for part of the decline in the national saving rate (and thus the rise in the current account deficit) in the past decade. Raising tax rates on the wealthy would solve this problem without injuring middle-class and working-class families who did not share much, if at all, in the upper-class "consumption binge" of the past decade.

The end of the Cold War should allow major reductions in military spending, especially if the temptation to revive or expand the United States' "global policeman" role in the aftermath of the Persian Gulf War can be avoided. Civilian public investment and educational expenditures, however,

> **Gradual measures to reduce the federal budget deficit . . . should focus first on restoring the progressivity of the tax system.**

130

should be exempted from budget cuts, and, if anything, need to be expanded in order to improve the nation's productivity and competitiveness (Aschauer, 1990).

In order to offset the contractionary effects of reducing the U.S. budget deficit, it is essential that interest rates be held down throughout the recovery period, and not raised prematurely. In addition, it is essential to continue the expansionary demand policies which most foreign countries followed in the late 1980s, and to restore economic growth in those areas which have lagged behind (especially Latin America). And finally, it is crucial for the dollar to be stabilized at a level which keeps U.S. products competitive in both foreign and domestic markets. This level will vary, however, according to the nature of U.S. trade problems with individual countries or country groups, as analyzed in this report.

Exchange rate policy should focus on keeping the dollar low and stable enough to keep U.S. exports to other industrial countries growing rapidly.

The dilemma facing U.S. policy is that the dollar needs to fall the most against those currencies whose exchange rates are managed, and which therefore cannot be directly influenced by the United States. These are the currencies of the supercompetitive NICs, particularly Korea and Taiwan. We have already argued that these nations should be induced to revalue their currencies to the point where their absolute advantages in unit labor costs in dollar terms are eliminated, with the threat of an equivalent import surcharge in case they do not revalue. In contrast, the U.S. can relatively easily depreciate the dollar against the European and Japanese currencies by unilaterally reducing U.S. interest rates (holding other factors constant). However, dollar depreciation has already largely eliminated the trade deficit with Europe, and has been relatively ineffective in reducing the trade deficit with Japan. With regard to all the industrialized countries, the post-1985 depreciation of the dollar seems to have done more to increase U.S. exports than to restrain U.S. imports.

Exchange rate policy should focus on keeping the dollar low and stable enough to keep U.S. exports to other industrial countries growing rapidly, as this is crucial for domestic employment growth, while other measures are used to influence underlying competitiveness. Ideally, target zones could be set for the exchange rates between the U.S. dollar and the other key currencies, especially the Japanese yen and the German deutschemark, as advocated by Williamson (1987) and Wachtel (1986), among others. Both interest rate policy and occasional foreign exchange market intervention could be used to keep actual rates within the target zones, and a credible commitment to accomplish this would do much to discourage destabilizing speculative runs.

If such international coordination of exchange rates cannot be arranged, then the U.S. should not hesitate to keep its own interest rates low and let the dollar fall somewhat, perhaps to the vicinity of 100 yen or 1.20 deutschemarks. Japan, Germany, and other industrialized countries might then be forced to lower their own interest rates, which would offset the dollar depreciation but contribute to greater global expansion of demand. This would be the opposite of what happened in the early 1980s, when other countries were forced to raise interest rates in response to tight U.S. monetary policy.

> **The most significant structural decline in the U.S. competitive position has occurred on the side of imports.**

However, the United States should not seek *continuous* dollar depreciation as a solution to its trade problems. In a world of highly integrated, speculative, and volatile financial markets, a continuous depreciation could easily turn into free fall. Moreover, excessive depreciation can lessen incentives for domestic producers to innovate and become more efficient, as observed by Porter (1990). And continuous depreciation (which raises import prices) can eventually feed into an inflationary spiral that would cut domestic real incomes, especially the wages of workers who lack indexing to inflation. The point, then, is not to encourage continuous depreciation, but to seek out and maintain a reasonably low level of the dollar. International cooperation in maintaining target zones would be the best way to achieve this, if other countries are willing to participate; we should be willing to trade off a slightly higher value of the dollar in exchange for such cooperation as it would make the task of exchange rate management easier and less risky. Unilateral action should be used as a last resort, however, and with the intention of inducing other countries to cooperate in practice even if a formal cooperative arrangement cannot be worked out.

Reviving Import-Competing Industries

The main empirical finding of this report is that the most significant structural decline in the U.S. competitive position has occurred on the side of imports. Our econometric analysis shows that U.S. exports have done about as well as could be expected given what has happened to foreign incomes and relative prices (including the effects of exchange rate changes). However, we have estimated that

U.S. nonoil imports have grown by about $98 billion more (in 1982 dollars, after correcting for the overvaluation of computers) over the past decade than would be expected from domestic expenditures and relative prices of imports. This finding naturally raises the question of whether any special type of aid to import-competing industries in the U.S. is justified.

Adoption of the complete policy package advocated here would do much to mitigate the problems of U.S. producers in import-competing sectors. The most rapidly growing source of manufactured imports is the East Asian NICs, and we have proposed either to eliminate their absolute advantage in unit labor costs or else to counteract it with an import surcharge. Japanese imports into the U.S. would also be subject to a surcharge, unless Japan made serious strides in raising its own imports of manufactures. Maintaining a reasonably low level of the dollar against industrial country currencies would help keep domestic products competitive in price terms with European and Japanese imports, while stabilizing exchange rates through target zones and policy coordination could help reduce the risk of future exchange rate "shocks." And emphasizing debt relief and renewed capital inflows rather than free trade agreements with Latin America would lessen the degree to which Latin America is forced to rely on low-wage exports to revive its growth.

The complete policy package advocated here would do much to mitigate the problems of U.S. producers in import-competing sectors.

Nevertheless, there may be some U.S. industries which will not be saved by these broad measures. These industries must be evaluated on a case-by-case basis to determine whether they warrant additional aid and, if so, what kind and with what conditions. The dominant consideration in offering such aid should be the potential for raising efficiency and restoring competitiveness. Only such potential can justify the costs of subsidizing or protecting industries which are currently uncompetitive. In some cases, only particular segments of an industry may be salvageable (e.g., specialty product lines with market niches). Industrial shrinkage or plant closings, where necessary, should be conducted in an orderly fashion, with notice to workers and communities, and with a serious and adequately funded program of adjustment assistance for displaced workers.

Economic theory teaches that in cases where there is a social benefit to be obtained from developing or modernizing an industry (such as spillovers to other industries, or reduced future production costs), the most efficient policy tool is a production subsidy rather than trade protection (tariff, quota, or VRA). Subsidies are less socially costly because they do not raise prices for consumers as trade policies do. Subsidies do not have to involve cash payments for goods produced, but can take more subtle forms such as preferential credit arrangements or funding for R&D activities.

For example, state and local governments currently provide numerous financial incentives for private investment, ranging from provision of infrastructure to tax holidays. Rather than having states and localities competing for investment, it would make more sense for the federal government to coordinate such efforts on the basis of national costs and benefits (see Luria, 1989, on the auto case). Another option would be the formation of an industrial development bank which could aid ailing industries, or at least a program of public loan guarantees on the Chrysler model (see Reich, 1988). Any such program would have to contain careful safeguards to make sure that the funds or credits were used only for the stated purpose of modernizing a particular industry. Performance targets (jobs, productivity growth, exports, etc.) should be set. Subsidies should be temporary (possibly through the use of credit) to avoid becoming a permanent crutch.

If subsidies cannot be implemented, then the next best policy is temporary trade protection. For this purpose, tariffs are preferable to quotas or VRAs. Tariffs generate revenue for the government, while quotas create scarcity "rents" for importers and—worst of all—VRAs give away the quota rents to foreign sellers (who can pocket the profits from the higher price in the U.S. market). Tariff protection should be offered only after careful cost-benefit analysis, taking account of the economic costs and social dislocation imposed by industries which shut down or move offshore, as well as the potential for increased efficiency in the protected industry. Protection should be given only in exchange for commitments to modernize and upgrade the industry. Extracting *quid pro quos* (in terms of reinvestment and modernization) from the firms which benefit is essential for obtaining net social benefits from such a program of temporary protection. It is especially important that some of the cost savings from modernization efforts be passed on to domestic consumers so as to minimize the adverse consequences of import restraints.

In the final analysis, however, such measures become necessary only as a result of years of neglect—neglect of

Protection should be offered only after careful cost-benefit analysis, [and] . . . in exchange for commitments to modernize and upgrade the industry.

134

domestic industrial development, neglect of foreign industrial targeting and trade practices, and neglect of sensible macroeconomic policies focused on real growth rather than financial interests. Aid to particular ailing industries, while sometimes necessary, cannot be the main basis for restoring U.S. competitiveness. The broad redesign of industrial, trade, and macro policies advocated here could enable the United States to balance its trade without excessive domestic hardships, and without relying on permanent trade protection in specific sectors.[10]

The broad redesign of industrial, trade, and macro policies advocated here could enable the United States to balance its trade without excessive domestic hardships.

Endnotes

1   According to the World Bank (1990, p. 181), Japan's GDP grew at an average annual rate of 6.5 percent from 1965–1980, compared with 2.7 percent in the United States. From 1980–88, however, Japan's growth rate fell to 3.9 percent, while the U.S. growth rate rose to 3.3 percent per year.

2   Any form of protection, whether a tariff (import duty) or quantitative restriction (such as a VRA), raises the domestic price of the good to some extent by creating an artificial scarcity in the importing country. This effect can be mitigated to some extent if the reduced imports help to drive down the world price, which can happen if the country is a "large" importer. In any case, protection creates a "wedge" between the world and domestic prices, and someone profits from this difference (sometimes called a "rent" by economists). In the case of a tariff, the home government captures the "rent" as tax revenue from the duty levied on imports. In the case of a VRA, however, the foreign firm which can sell its allotted exports at a higher price in the home market pockets the "rent" as excess profits.

3   This "sterilization" is done by selling off other central bank assets (such as domestic government bonds) while foreign exchange reserves are accumulating, so as to keep total central bank assets from rising too fast. This must be done because the base of the domestic money supply consists of the liabilities of the central bank (currency plus reserve deposits of commercial banks), which must be equal to its assets. If assets are allowed to grow too fast, so must liabilities, which could be inflationary.

4   Note that this avoids the problem of the so-called "scientific tariff," which is designed to equalize *wages*. There is no need for wages to be equal, if wage differentials between countries are proportional to (average) productivity differentials. The point of the present proposal is precisely to force wage differentials in dollar terms to be proportional to average productivity differentials. Note that this would still leave the NICs with *comparative* advantages in those goods in which their relative productivity exceeds their relative wage rate, as in classical trade theory (see Dornbusch, Fischer, and Samuelson, 1977).

5   For example, there is now a labor rights provision under the U.S. General System of Preferences (GSP) for imports from LDCs. The countries which have been cited under this provision have included Nicaragua (under the Sandinistas), Romania (under Ceausescu), Paraguay (under Stroessner), and Chile (under Pinochet). Countries which have been found in compliance include Guatemala, Haiti, the Philippines, South Korea, Taiwan, Thailand, Turkey, and Israel—all U.S. allies.

6   Greater debt relief for Latin America could be phased in gradually in order to minimize the impact on currently vulnerable banks. The banks could be given new instruments with more realistic (written down) face values and more feasible repayment schedules in order to enhance the quality of their remaining assets.

7   This paragraph draws upon the ideas of Dernburg (1989).

[8] See Lustig (1990b) on the inadequacy of the Brady Plan debt relief negotiated for Mexico, and United Nations Economic Commission for Latin America and the Caribbean (UN/ECLAC, 1990) for a broader critique.

[9] In fact, we may already be close to achieving the first goal. The federal debt held by the public stabilized at about 42 percent of GNP in 1987-1989, after rising from about 26 percent in 1980-1981. Although this percentage subsequently rose to 44 percent in 1990, this increase could be temporary due to the recession. However, the total federal debt (including the part held by federal trust funds) has risen continuously from about 33 percent in 1980-1981 to 50 percent in 1986 and nearly 59 percent in 1990. The reason for this discrepancy is that rising on-budget deficits are increasingly being financed by off-budget surpluses (mostly from increases in the social security trust fund). Economically, however, it is the net federal debt outstanding to the public which really matters in relation to how much the federal government has had to borrow to cover its total fiscal deficits (on- and off-budget together).

[10] It may still be necessary to manage trade in specific sectors on a more or less permanent basis in order to deal with problems of global excess capacity or in order to harmonize industrial and trade policies across countries, as argued by Kuttner (1989). But managed trade in this sense is not a device for balancing trade at the macro level.

137

Appendix:
Econometric Estimates
of U.S. Import and
Export Demand

This Appendix presents the estimates of import and export demand functions for the United States which are used to derive some of the results reported in Chapter 3. In particular, the new estimates of the income elasticities of import and export demand, the trend deterioration in competitiveness on the side of imports, and the cumulative increase in imports due to "structural" factors are all based on the econometric regressions reported here. The method for estimating the structural trend in competitiveness presumes that all the effects of standard macro policies (fiscal, monetary, and exchange rate) as well as saving-investment behavior operate through relative income and price effects. If, after controlling for these effects, there is also a statistically significant time trend, then this implies that some structural factors (other than the standard macro policies and saving-investment behavior) have an independent effect on the balance of trade.[1]

An obvious problem in econometric studies of import and export demand (which is evident from Table 4 in the text) is that different specifications of the demand functions, different ways of measuring the variables, different sample periods, and different econometric techniques can lead to widely varying results. We have not attempted to duplicate all the earlier results of other authors. Nevertheless, we do test the *sensitivity* of our own results to these types of differences by systematically comparing a number of alternative specifications. For this reason, the present study compares the results for two different sample periods (1975–1989 and 1980–89) and with a variety of alternative measures of relative prices and national incomes (or expenditures). Also, the equations are estimated with the variables measured in both levels and first differences of natural logarithms. The former specification (log levels) is more comparable with previous studies, while the latter (log differences) yields more unbiased tests for the statistical significance of the estimated parameters. In both specifications, the estimated coefficients on the price and income variables can be interpreted as elasticities.

This econometric exercise requires a number of choices about how to measure the variables. The first choice concerns the measure of relative prices. Figure A-1 shows three alternative measures of relative import prices for nonoil commodities. For each measure, the denominator is the BLS producer price index for nonfuel industrial commodities (PPINF), used to represent the domestic prices of internationally traded U.S. goods.[2] For the numerator, one commonly used measure of import prices is the implicit price deflator for nonpetroleum merchandise imports from the national income and product accounts (NIPAs).[3] The ratio of this import deflator to PPINF is presented as the solid line in Figure A-1.

The problems with the implicit deflator measure of import prices can be seen by comparing Figure A-1 with Figure 8 (in the text). In making this comparison, it should be noted that the real value of the U.S. dollar as defined in Figure 8 measures the relative price of domestic goods to foreign goods, while the relative import price in Figure A-1 is the *inverse* ratio. Thus, if relative import prices follow the real exchange rate, we should expect the former to fall when the latter rises, and conversely. From 1980–85, when the dollar rose substantially by either measure of the real exchange rate in Figure 8, the relative price of imports (measured by the deflator in Figure A-1) fell sharply, as we would expect. However, while the real exchange rate indexes show the dollar falling in 1985–88 about as much as it rose in 1980–85, the relative price of imports (measured by the deflator) rises only slightly in 1985–86, then flattens out in 1987–88, and falls again in 1989—to *below* the 1985

Figure A-1
Alternative Measures of the Relative Price of
Nonoil Imports, Quarterly 1973-1989

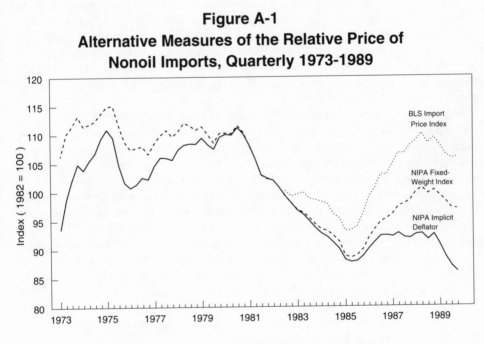

Sources: Department of Commerce, BEA; Department of Labor, BLS; and author's calculations.
Note: See text for explanation.

level. According to this measure, then, the massive dollar depreciation of the last five years had no lasting effect in improving the price competitiveness of U.S. goods relative to imports.

One reason for this discrepancy could be the "pass-through" problem. When foreign exporters are confronted with a depreciation of the dollar (appreciation of their home currency), they are faced with a loss of revenue in their own currency. If foreign firms raise the dollar prices of their exports by the same percentage as the dollar has fallen, their export volumes will fall as U.S. consumers switch away from the more expensive foreign goods (how much, depends on the price elasticity). This response is called full (100 percent) pass-through. At the other extreme, foreign sellers can choose to hold their dollar prices constant in order to preserve their market share in the United States, thus accepting lower prices in their home currencies (and hence reduced profit margins over their domestic costs of production). This option would be zero pass-through. Obviously, it is also possible to choose an intermediate response by passing on anywhere between 0 and 100 percent of the exchange-rate change in higher dollar prices. Some studies have found an unusually low degree of exchange-rate pass-through into U.S. import prices (usually measured by the implicit deflator) after the dollar fell in 1985 (see Mann, 1986; Helkie and Hooper, 1988; Hooper and Mann, 1989a). But others (e.g., Lawrence, 1990) have argued that the apparently low pass-through rate is due to the difficulties of measuring computer prices in recent years. While it is not necessary to resolve this debate for present purposes, it is important to consider how it affects our analysis.

In order to understand how computer prices affect the implicit deflator for imports, it is useful to recall how an implicit deflator is calculated: it is the ratio of the nominal value of goods (in current prices) to their "real" value (in constant 1982 prices). The calculation of the "real" value of computer imports raises some difficult issues, however. The U.S. NIPAs use what is called a "hedonic" measure of computer output. That is, each computer is evaluated as a bundle of attributes, such as memory capacity, processing speed, and printing power. The "real" value of each attribute is then assumed to be its 1982 price, since 1982 is the base year for real output in the NIPAs. The implicit deflator for computers is actually based on the data series for computer *investment*; this same deflator is then applied to the values of computer imports and exports to estimate the "real" volume of computer imports and exports (Lawrence, 1990).

Without entering into the thorny question of whether the hedonic method is appropriate in principle (see Denison, 1989; and Young, 1989), it is clear that the use of 1982 prices severely distorts the results of using this method. The personal computer revolution was still in its infancy in 1982, and many computer attributes which are now standard and cheap were then prohibitively expensive. As more powerful personal computers become cheaper, consumers buy (and import) more of them. Since their "real" value is calculated in 1982 prices, the real quantity of computers for subsequent years is exaggerated, and *the computer price deflator (which is rapidly falling) acquires an exaggerated (and* increasing) *weight in the overall import deflator.* Moreover, this distortion increases as we get farther in time from 1982. This problem will largely disappear when the NIPAs are converted to a 1987 base for calculating "real" magnitudes, but the 1987-based NIPA data will not be available until November 1991 (see U.S. Congressional Budget Office, 1990, for a preview).

Fortunately, there is an alternative measure of import prices which can be calculated from the existing NIPAs: a *fixed-weight price index.* This measure shows the current cost of buying the base-year (1982) mix of imports. While this measure also uses the hedonic approach to measuring computer prices, and thus shows a rapid decline in those prices after 1982, *it does not give computers an ever-increasing weight in the average price level as the implicit deflator does.* The ratio of the fixed weight index for nonpetroleum imports[4] to PPINF is shown as the dashed line in Figure A-1. Note that this measure shows a much more substantial response of import prices to the fall in the dollar after 1985 than the implicit deflator, although the post-1985 rise in import prices is still just about half of the pre-1985 fall.

Since the third quarter of 1982, another measure of average import prices has been published by the Bureau of Labor Statistics (BLS). The BLS index of import prices (based on 1985 weights) for all commodities excluding energy, relative to PPINF, is drawn as the dotted line in Figure A-1. According to the BLS index, there was a very substantial increase in the relative price of imports from 1985 to 1988, even greater than what the NIPA fixed weight index shows. The higher level of the BLS index is mainly accounted for by a different (nonhedonic) method of treating computer prices (see Alterman, 1991). Unfortunately, since the BLS index was not calculated before the third quarter of 1982, we cannot use it to draw any inferences about how the 1985–88 increase compares with the 1980–85 decrease.

For the econometric analysis, the NIPA fixed-weight index of import prices is preferred. This measure avoids the problem of continuously increasing weights for computers which contaminates the NIPA implicit price deflator, and is available for a longer period than the BLS index. Moreover, the NIPA fixed-weight index traces an intermediate path between the other two alternatives for the post-1985 period, indicating that it avoids some of the more extreme biases which may be built into them.

In addition to this direct measure of the relative price of imports, we can also use the (reciprocals of the) two real exchange rate indexes shown in Figure 8 in the text: the official Federal Reserve Board index of the real value of the dollar against the G-10 currencies, and the Dallas Fed RX-101 index covering 101 nations. By comparing our results using these two indexes with our results using the import price index, we can gauge the sensitivity of our results to the choice of a relative price variable, and also test for the importance of the limited pass-through problem.

It is also necessary to choose an income variable for the import demand equation. Most studies measure income with a domestic expenditure variable. In the U.S. NIPAs, the relevant series is called "gross domestic purchases," which equals the sum of personal consumption expenditures, gross domestic investment, and government purchases. This variable measures the total level of demand in the country (what economic theorists call "absorption"), regardless of whether it is spent on domestic or foreign products.

Helkie and Hooper (1988) argue that gross national product (GNP) is preferable, since many imports are intermediate goods used in production rather than final goods devoted to consumption or investment. However, there are two flaws in their argument. First, the best measure of production in a country would actually be the gross *domestic* product (GDP), not the GNP, which includes net factor income from abroad. Moreover, GNP includes the effects of trade surpluses (which raise it) or deficits (which lower it),[5] which raises a question as to whether it is truly an exogenous variable with respect to the demand for imports. Given that opinion is divided on which variable is preferable, I use both GNP and domestic expenditures in the import equations. As will be seen below, the results are generally similar for the two measures.

To measure the volume of imports, real nonpetroleum imports in 1982 dollars is used as the dependent variable. Based on the above discussion of the problems with the NIPA implicit deflator for nonpetroleum imports due to the use of 1982 prices as weights for computer attributes, we must recognize an upward bias in the associated NIPA measure of real nonpetroleum imports. Indeed, it is the upward bias in real imports which causes the downward bias in the implicit deflator. Unfortunately, no valid alternative measure of real imports is presently available.[6] Since all recent studies use the 1982 dollar "real" import series, our results will at least be comparable to those other studies.

In any event, the work of Meade (1990) indicates that only a small bias is introduced by the presence of computers in the real import variable. We can use her results to estimate the degree to which our estimates are affected by the problem of computer prices. Using Helkie and Hooper's (1988) specification of the import demand function, she obtains similar results for nonpetroleum imports both excluding and including computers. As discussed in regard to Table 4 in the text, this specification essentially captures the time trend in a "relative supply" term: the ratio of the capital stock in the U.S. to foreign capital stocks. The coefficient on this variable drops only from -0.90 to -0.74 when computers are excluded from the dependent variable. (Since the relative supply term falls secularly, the negative coefficients indicate a rising tendency of U.S. imports.) Since 0.74 is about 82 percent of 0.90, we may infer that only 18 percent of the secular rise in imports is accounted for by computers—and some part of that 18 percent is undoubtedly genuine (not due to the problems with the implicit deflator).

The import demand regressions are presented in Tables A-1 through A-4. All the equations were estimated using ordinary least squares (OLS). Table A-1 gives the results for quarterly regressions from 1975:1 to 1989:4, with the variables measured in log levels and a linear time trend. A constant term was included but is not shown in the table for reasons of space. The coefficients for the relative price variables are all sums for a 0–8 quarter distributed lag. Some of the specifications (particularly those using domestic expenditures as the income variable) show significant positive time trends. In equation 1.12, which has the best fit (and highest Durbin-Watson), this trend is about 0.3 percent per quarter, or about 1.2 percent per year.

All the equations in Table A-1 have a high degree of autocorrelation of the residuals, as indicated by low Durbin-Watson (D.W.) statistics (with 60 observations and eleven variables including lags in the regressions with a time trend, the 5 percent lower and upper bounds of the D.W. statistic are 1.184 and 2.031, respectively).[7] Autocorrelation of the residuals makes the statistical significance tests based on ordinary least

TABLE A-1
Nonpetroleum Import Demand Equations, Quarterly 1975:1—1989:4
Variables Measured in Levels of Natural Logarithms

| Equation Number | Relative Price of Imports | | | U.S. National Income | | Time Trend | $\bar{R}^2$ | Durbin-Watson |
	G-10 Index	RX-101 Index	Fixed Weight Index	GNP	Expenditures			
1.1	−0.57***			3.02***			0.992	0.965
1.2	−0.52***			2.51***		0.004**	0.992	0.962
1.3	−0.33***				2.89***		0.993	0.984
1.4	−0.31***				2.20***	0.005***	0.995	1.261
1.5		−0.87***		2.86***			0.991	0.867
1.6		−0.84***		2.64***		0.002	0.991	0.839
1.7		−0.50***			2.80***		0.993	1.044
1.8		−0.47***			2.28***	0.004***	0.995	1.154
1.9			−1.57***	2.44***			0.992	0.941
1.10			−1.57***	2.45***		0.000	0.992	0.941
1.11			−0.97***		2.56***		0.994	1.195
1.12			−0.90***		2.18***	0.003***	0.995	1.296

* Significant at the 10 percent level (one-tail test).
** Significant at the 5 percent level (one-tail test).
*** Significant at the 1 percent level (one-tail test).

Note: A constant term was included in each equation but is not reported here. All equations were estimated by ordinary least squares (OLS). The coefficients on the prices are the sums for lags 0-8.

TABLE A-2
Nonpetroleum Import Demand Equations, Quarterly 1975:2—1989:4
Variables Measured in First Differences of Natural Logarithms

Equation Number	Relative Price of Imports			U.S. National Income		Constant	$\bar{R}^2$	Durbin-Watson
	G-10 Index	RX-101 Index	Fixed Weight Index	GNP	Expenditures			
2.1	−0.37**			2.17***			0.229	2.088
2.2	−0.36**			1.53***		0.012**	0.286	2.043
2.3	−0.18				2.22***		0.362	2.146
2.4	−0.21				1.78***	0.009**	0.393	2.159
2.5		−0.63**		2.13***			0.167	1.995
2.6		−0.59*		1.50***		0.012**	0.220	1.920
2.7		−0.31			2.19***		0.291	2.077
2.8		−0.35			1.74***	0.009**	0.320	2.052
2.9			−1.92***	1.69***			0.211	2.355
2.10			−1.64***	1.14**		0.010**	0.244	2.273
2.11			−1.36**		1.82***		0.295	2.457
2.12			−1.22**		1.41***	0.009*	0.320	2.450

* Significant at the 10 percent level (one-tail test).
** Significant at the 5 percent level (one-tail test).
*** Significant at the 1 percent level (one-tail test).

Note: All equations were estimated by OLS. The coefficients on the relative prices are the sums for lags 0-8.

145

squares (OLS) estimation invalid; it also makes the OLS coefficient estimates inefficient. These results are thus presented mainly for comparison with previous studies.

To address the autocorrelation problem, the equations were re-run in first differences of logs (which approximate percentage changes).[8] The sample period then starts in 1975:2 in order to have 8 lags of the G-10 real exchange rate index available. In the regressions in first differences of logs, shown in Table A-2, the constant term captures the time trend (since it measures the constant part of the quarterly percentage *change* in import demand).

The constant terms are significant at the 5 percent level in five of the six equations in which a constant is included in Table A-2, and at the 10 percent level in the sixth. The implied rates of change are more than double the estimated time trends in the log-level regressions, averaging about 1 percent per quarter or roughly 4 percent per year. Although the statistical significance appears lower[9] with log differences, it should be recalled that the degree of significance was exaggerated in the log-level regressions due to the presence of autocorrelated residuals. Note that the D.W. statistics in Table A-2 are all close to 2.0 or higher; eleven out of the twelve are above the 5 percent upper bound (about 1.99 for fifty-nine observations and ten variables), and the other one is just below it. Thus the first difference specification shows no significant first order autocorrelation of the residuals, which implies that it provides more reliable significance tests. The results in Table A-2 therefore give us additional confidence that there has been a structural rising tendency of real imports over the last fifteen years, at a rate of roughly 4 percent per year.

Table A-3 shows the results of estimating import demand in log levels for the period 1980:1 to 1989:4 only. For the decade of the 1980s, the time trends are consistently positive (about 0.4 to 0.7 percent per quarter, or 1.6 to 2.8 percent per year) and appear significant at the 1 percent level in all but one equation (where the trend is significant at the 5 percent level). However, once again the low D.W. statistics imply that the statistical significance of these estimates may be exaggerated and that the estimates themselves are inefficient. Table A-4 therefore gives the results of estimating the 1980s regressions in log differences. Again, the constant terms show consistently positive and somewhat higher time trends (0.8 to 1.0 percent per quarter, or 3.2 to 4.0 percent per year), with apparently lower significance levels (mostly 10 percent)—but we can have more confidence in these estimates due to the absence of autocorrelation of the residuals. (Note that *all* the D.W.'s in Table A-4 are above the 5 percent upper bound of 2.149 for forty observations and ten regressors.)

Given the problem of limited pass-through of dollar depreciation into import prices discussed earlier, it is interesting to compare the estimated time trends (or constant terms in first differences) in the regressions with the fixed-weight import-price index and those with the two exchange rate indexes. If significant time trends appeared only in the equations with exchange rate indexes, but not in the equations with the import price index, then those trends would merely be capturing the pass-through problem. In fact, the estimated time trends in the equations using import prices are only slightly lower than in the corresponding equations using exchange rates in every case, indicating that partial pass-through accounts for only a small part of the secular increase in U.S. imports. The consistently positive estimates of the time

TABLE A-3
Nonpetroleum Import Demand Equations, Quarterly 1980:1—1989:4
Variables Measured in Levels of Natural Logarithms

Equation Number	Relative Price of Imports			U.S. National Income		Time Trend	$\bar{R}^2$	Durbin-Watson
	G-10 Index	RX-101 Index	Fixed Weight Index	GNP	Expenditures			
3.1	−0.53***			3.12***			0.988	1.014
3.2	−0.49***			2.25***		0.007***	0.992	1.304
3.3	−0.27***				2.84***		0.990	1.038
3.4	−0.29***				2.10***	0.006***	0.993	1.371
3.5		−0.92***		2.92***			0.989	1.072
3.6		−0.84***		2.18***		0.006***	0.991	1.226
3.7		−0.46***			2.76***		0.990	1.120
3.8		−0.49***			2.10***	0.006***	0.993	1.343
3.9			−1.57***	2.59***			0.990	1.104
3.10			−1.48***	2.08***		0.004**	0.991	1.157
3.11			−0.85***		2.58***		0.992	1.176
3.12			−0.89***		2.06***	0.005***	0.993	1.278

* Significant at the 10 percent level (one-tail test).
** Significant at the 5 percent level (one-tail test).
*** Significant at the 1 percent level (one-tail test).

Note: A constant term was included in each equation but is not reported here. All equations were estimated by OLS. The coefficients on the prices are the sums for lags 0-8.

TABLE A-4
Nonpetroleum Import Demand Equations, Quarterly 1980:1—1989:4
Variables Measured in First Differences of Natural Logarithms

Equation Number	Relative Price of Imports			U.S. National Income		Constant	$\bar{R}^2$	Durbin-Watson
	G-10 Index	RX-101 Index	Fixed Weight Index	GNP	Expenditures			
4.1	−0.35**			2.37***			0.200	2.281
4.2	−0.31*			1.88***		0.009*	0.242	2.226
4.3	−0.15				2.29***		0.312	2.287
4.4	−0.14				1.91***	0.009*	0.347	2.309
4.5		−0.69**		2.20***			0.165	2.286
4.6		−0.58*		1.69***		0.010*	0.213	2.229
4.7		−0.31			2.23***		0.270	2.303
4.8		−0.28			1.82***	0.009*	0.310	2.322
4.9			−1.44**	2.05***			0.182	2.543
4.10			−1.23**	1.66***		0.008	0.194	2.501
4.11			−0.88*		2.06***		0.279	2.604
4.12			−0.72		1.74***	0.008*	0.302	2.645

* Significant at the 10 percent level (one-tail test).
** Significant at the 5 percent level (one-tail test).
*** Significant at the 1 percent level (one-tail test).

Note: All equations were estimated using ordinary least squares. The coefficients on the relative prices are the sums for lags 0–8.

trend in the import demand equations in Tables A-1 to A-4, along with the reasonable magnitudes of the estimates, give us some confidence that such a trend truly exists, in spite of the varying "significance levels."[10]

The discussion of the cumulative decline in U.S. competitiveness (structural increase in imports) in Chapter 3 is based on equation 4.12 in Table A-4. This equation was chosen for a number of reasons: the use of first differences avoids autocorrelated residuals, the use of the expenditure variable is theoretically more appealing than the GNP variable (although in practice this choice turns out to make little difference), the fixed weight index is the most reliable measure of import prices, and the 1980–89 sample period incorporates only information from the past decade. No part of the structural trend estimated by this equation can be attributed to limited pass-through, since an import price index is used rather than an exchange rate index. Moreover, the estimated trend rate of increase in imports of 0.8 percent per quarter (about 3.2 percent per year) is around the middle of the range of estimates reported in Tables A-1 to A-4. And as discussed earlier, Meade's (1990) results give us confidence that only a small part of the trend can be attributed to the mismeasurement of "real" computer imports.

To calculate the cumulative impact of the structural rising tendency of U.S. imports (the $106.6 billion figure cited in Chapter 3 and text Table 5 for 1980–89), the following procedure was used. First, the fitted values from equation (4.12) were obtained. Since the equation was run in log differences, the fitted values from the regression are estimated proportional changes in nonpetroleum imports for 1980:1 to 1989:4. These changes were then applied to actual imports in 1979:4 to generate a series of fitted values for the level of imports over the next forty quarters (ten years). Then, the same equation was simulated under the counterfactual assumption that the time trend (constant term in the log-difference regression) was zero, with the same coefficients on the other variables. This counterfactual simulation generated an estimate of the part of the proportional changes in imports which is explained by changes in relative prices and U.S. national income. These changes were applied to actual imports from 1979:4 to generate a series for what imports would have been in 1980:1 to 1989:4 if there had *not* been a structural rising tendency. Finally, I took the *difference* between the fitted values for the level of imports and the simulated imports without a structural trend for each quarter. The $106.6 billion figure is the average difference for the four quarters of 1989.

The estimates of export demand functions are presented in Tables A-5 and A-6 for the log-level and log-difference regressions, respectively. Without a much larger model disaggregated by countries, there is no way to calculate a true relative price of U.S. exports *in foreign markets* analogous to the relative price of U.S. imports (fixed-weight index) used in the import demand regressions. Nevertheless, the real exchange rate indexes at least reflect consumer prices indexes (CPIs) in foreign countries relative to the U.S. Therefore, we can obtain an index of the ratio of U.S. export prices (in foreign currency) to foreign consumer prices by multiplying the implicit price deflator for nonagricultural exports (from the U.S. NIPAs) by each of the two real exchange rate indexes, and then dividing the products by the U.S. CPI.

TABLE A-5
Nonagricultural Export Equations, Quarterly 1975:1—1989:4 and 1980:1—1989:4
Variables Measured In Levels of Natural Logarithms

Equation Number	Sample Period	Relative Price[a]		Foreign Income		Time Trend	$\overline{R}^2$	Durbin-Watson
		G-10 Index	RX-101 Index	Rest of World	Other OECD			
5.1	1975–89	−0.72***		1.27***			0.972	0.430
5.2	1975–89	−0.71***		1.37***		−0.001	0.972	0.432
5.3	1975–89		−1.20***	1.16***			0.963	0.348
5.4	1975–89		−1.11***	2.11***		−0.007*	0.964	0.381
5.5	1975–89	−0.71***			1.50***		0.975	0.483
5.6	1975–89	−0.70***			1.75***	−0.002	0.975	0.496
5.7	1980–89	−0.70***		1.31***			0.960	0.305
5.8	1980–89	−0.15**		7.93***	−0.050***		0.986	1.965
5.9	1980–89		1.26***	0.85***			0.953	0.270
5.10	1980–89		−0.24*	8.10***		−0.053***	0.984	1.834
5.11	1980–89	−0.69***			1.56**		0.968	0.324
5.12	1980–89	−0.38***			5.77***	−0.028***	0.989	1.821

[a]Each index of the value of the U.S. dollar was multiplied by the ratio of the implicit price deflator for nonagricultural exports to the U.S. consumer price index.
* Significant at the 10 percent level (one-tail test).
** Significant at the 5 percent level (one-tail test).
*** Significant at the 1 percent level (one-tail test).

Note: A constant term was included in each equation but is not reported here. All equations were estimated by OLS. The coefficients on the prices are the sums for lags 0—8. Foreign income is measured by real GDP in 1985 dollars.

TABLE A-6
Nonagricultural Export Equations, Quarterly 1975:2—1989:4 and 1980:1—1989:4
Variables Measured in First Differences of Natural Logarithms

Equation Number	Sample Period	Relative Price[a] G-10 Index	Relative Price[a] RX-101 Index	Foreign Income Rest of World	Foreign Income Other OECD	Constant	$\overline{R}^2$	Durbin-Watson
6.1	1975–89	−0.76***		1.16***			0.285	1.839
6.2	1975–89	−0.78***		0.64		0.005	0.276	1.777
6.3	1975–89		−1.24***	1.00**			0.222	1.732
6.4	1975–89		−1.25***	0.75		0.003	0.207	1.697
6.5	1975–89	−0.77***			1.23***		0.290	1.934
6.6	1975–89	−0.78***			0.75	0.005	0.285	1.845
6.7	1980–89	−0.73***		1.37***			0.424	1.556
6.8	1980–89	−0.72***		1.65*		−0.003	0.405	1.604
6.9	1980–89		−1.30***	0.98**			0.350	1.545
6.10	1980–89		−1.27***	1.36		−0.003*	0.330	1.605
6.11	1980–89	−0.70***			1.76***		0.494	1.758
6.12	1980–89	−0.69***			2.05**	−0.003	0.481	1.853

[a]Each index of the value of the U.S. dollar was multiplied by the ratio of the implicit price deflator for nonagricultural exports to the U.S. consumer price index.

* Significant at the 10 percent level (one-tail test).

** Significant at the 5 percent level (one-tail test).

*** Significant at the 1 percent level (one-tail test).

Note: All equations were estimated by OLS. The coefficients on the relative prices are the sums for lags 0–8. Foreign income is measured by real GDP in 1985 dollars.

This reliance on the implicit price deflator for U.S. exports and the real exchange rate indexes is not likely to bias the results for our export equation. Experiments showed that using the fixed-weight price index for nonagricultural exports yields qualitatively similar results to those obtained using the implicit deflator, with slightly worse fits (as indicated by lower R^2's in comparable specifications). As for the real exchange rate indexes, the RX-101 index may appear superior to the G-10 index because the former includes more countries with which the U.S. trades. However, it should be recalled that U.S. exports compete mainly with Japanese, German, and other industrialized country exports in third markets. For this reason, the G-10 index is also relevant, and actually generates slightly better fits (higher R^2's).

Another difficulty with the export equation is the problem of finding reliable measures of foreign income (or expenditures) on a quarterly basis. Quarterly national income accounts for the other OECD countries (Western Europe plus Canada, Japan, Australia, New Zealand, and Turkey) are available from 1975 to the present. From these accounts, we can calculate non-U.S. real GDP in constant 1985 dollars.[11] There is no reason to believe that using foreign GDP rather than GNP or expenditures will make a significant difference to the results, since the discrepancies between these variables are minuscule relative to total rest-of-world income.

Roughly 40 percent of U.S. exports go to developing countries. Quarterly data on developing country GDP are not generally available. Therefore, I took the annual real GDP index for the developing countries from the International Monetary Fund, *International Financial Statistics*, and used it to interpolate quarterly data.[12] The actual quarterly data for the other OECD countries and the interpolated quarterly data for the developing countries were then combined into a weighted average index, with weights of 0.6 and 0.4, respectively (based roughly on average 1980s shares of U.S. exports).

This admittedly crude index of foreign GDP understates the degree of cyclical volatility of rest-of-world income, due to the need to interpolate developing country quarterly GDP (although rest-of-world GDP is naturally smoothed to some extent by the aggregation of GDPs for different countries with nonsynchronized business cycles). More seriously, this index may give undue weight to some countries which are relatively closed to U.S. exports, since it is not constructed using U.S. export weights.[13] For this reason, the export demand equations were also estimated using other OECD GDP alone as a proxy for foreign income. This alternative may be justified by: (1) the fact that the OECD accounts for most U.S. exports; (2) the fact that OECD quarterly GDP is more accurately measured; and (3) the view that developing country growth is largely dependent on industrial country growth (Taylor, 1983).

Although the data series used in the export equations may be less reliable for the reasons just indicated, the results seem reasonable in comparison with previous studies. The regressions presented in Tables A-5 and A-6 all use real nonagricultural exports in 1982 dollars as the dependent variable.[14] A negative time trend (or constant term with first differences) in these regressions would represent a secular decline in competitiveness. Regression results are given for both exchange rate indexes with rest-of-world GDP, and for the G-10 index only with other OECD GDP.[15]

In all the export regressions run *without* time trends (or constants in first differences), the estimated income elasticities are well below the corresponding income elasticities of import demand shown in Tables A-1 to A-4. Thus our results confirm the traditional Houthakker-Magee findings, also corroborated more recently by Cline (1989) and Lawrence (1990), which were discussed in regard to Table 4 in Chapter 3.

Negative time trends are found for exports in 1975-1989 when the equations are estimated in log levels (top half of Table A-5), but they are not statistically significant (except with the RX-101 index, at the 10 percent level). When the export regressions are run in log levels for the 1980s only (bottom half of Table A-5), we obtain what appear to be large and significant negative time trends. But these estimated time trends are unbelievably large: − 5.0, − 5.3, and − 2.8 percent *per quarter* in equations 5.8, 5.10, and 5.12, respectively. Also, the estimated foreign-income elasticities rise to implausible levels when the time trend is added to these equations (the same result was reported by Krugman and Baldwin, 1987, with a different sample period and data set). This implies that the estimated negative time trends for exports in 1980−89 are probably exaggerated at best.

The most likely reason for these spurious results is multicollinearity between the log of foreign GDP and the linear time trend. Both the aggregation of real GDP for so many countries and the interpolation of quarterly GDP for the developing countries (in the regressions using rest-of-world GDP) contribute to a very smooth overall index, which rises at a rather constant rate for the last fifteen years (except for a slowdown in 1980−82). Multicollinearity of foreign GDP (in logs) and the time trend makes it impossible to separate the effects of these two variables. Hence the estimated time trends for exports are not reliable.

When we run the export equations in first differences of logs, we obtain positive but insignificant time trends (constant terms) for 1975−1989 (top half of Table A-6), and negative but mostly insignificant time trends (constants) for 1980−89 only (bottom half of Table A-6). Comparing equations 6.8, 6.10, and 6.12 with 5.8, 5.10, and 5.12, we do not find the perverse behavior of the estimated income elasticities in the regressions in log differences that we found in the log-level regressions. This suggests that differencing removed the multicollinearity problem. The results for the export equations thus provide at best very weak evidence that there may have been a declining trend of U.S. exports in 1980−89, apart from the effects of changes in relative prices, exchange rates, and foreign income growth. The safest conclusion, however, is that the structural deterioration in U.S. competitiveness was felt mainly by the import-competing sectors of the economy.

Endnotes to Appendix

1   This is the same method that was used by Krugman and Baldwin (1987), but our results are different—especially for import demand, where we find consistent evidence for a significant positive time trend.

2   Similar results are obtained when other producer price indexes (e.g., for finished goods excluding energy) are used. A producer price index is preferred to the GNP deflator because the former better expresses the price level for traded goods, while the latter includes many nontraded services.

3   This measure is used by Helkie and Hooper (1988), among others.

4   Table 7.15 of the NIPAs gives fixed weight price indices for merchandise imports. Although the average index for nonpetroleum imports is not given, it can easily be calculated from the formula:

$$P_{mt} = \alpha_{82} P_{nt} + (1 - \alpha_{82}) P_{pt}$$

where α_{82} is the share of nonpetroleum imports in total merchandise imports in the base year 1982; P_{mt} is the price index for all merchandise imports, P_{nt} is the price index for nonpetroleum imports, and P_{pt} is the price index for petroleum imports (all in quarter t). Since all the other data besides P_{nt} are known, this variable can be solved for.

5   GNP is defined as consumption + investment + government purchases + (exports − imports). Gross domestic purchases is just the sum of consumption + investment + government purchases.

6   Dividing nominal imports by the fixed-weight price index would yield the *purchasing power* of current import expenditures over the 1982 basket of imports, but this would not be a true index of import quantities. Lawrence (1990) simply excludes computers from the real import and export series, but this seems inappropriate since computers are an important part of U.S. trade.

7   If the D.W. statistic is above the upper bound, then the null hypothesis of no serial correlation of the residuals can be accepted. If the D.W. statistic is below the lower bound, then this null hypothesis must be rejected. If the D.W. statistic is in between the upper and lower bounds, then we are uncertain as to whether the null hypothesis can be accepted or rejected.

8   Simply estimating the equations in log levels with a correction for first-order autocorrelation (AR1) did not yield good results. The estimated "rho" coefficients were generally insignificant.

9   In the rather confusing terminology of statistical significance tests, a *higher* significance "level" (percentage) means a *lower* degree of significance (i.e., less confidence that the coefficient is truly different from zero). For example, if a coefficient estimate is "significant at the 10 percent level" this means that we have a 10 percent chance of having falsely rejected the null hypothesis that the coefficient

equals zero; whereas if the estimate is "significant at the 1 percent level" this means that we have only a 1 percent chance of having made such an error. In any case, these levels are only reliable under certain conditions, including the absence of serial correlation of the least squares residuals.

[0] Although Krugman and Baldwin (1987, Table 3, p. 19) failed to find such a positive time trend in their import equations, it should be noted that they used a different sample period (1977:2 to 1986:4). We find such a trend both for the longer period 1975–1989 and for the 1980s alone.

[1] Real GDP is measured in each country's own currency for some base year, and then converted to dollars at 1985 exchange rates. While the dollar was at a record high in that year, the other currencies were not seriously misaligned with each other. Thus the use of 1985 exchange rates does not give undue weight to any particular other country. Also, since we are only interested in the proportional changes in real foreign GDP, the dollar level of foreign GDP is irrelevant.

[2] The interpolation was performed assuming that each quarter's GDP was a five-quarter moving average of the annual figures. I used the following (arbitrary) weights:

First quarter = 0.4(previous year) + 0.6(current year)
Second quarter = 0.2(previous year) + 0.8(current year)
Third quarter = 0.8(current year) + 0.2(following year)
Fourth quarter = 0.6(current year) + 0.4(following year).

Since the annual series is only available through 1988, the 1989 developing country real GDP index was forecast using IMF growth forecasts.

[3] It could be argued, however, that it is better to measure the true sensitivity of U.S. exports to total foreign incomes (excluding only the centrally planned economies) rather than to give a lower weight to countries with closed markets, as the conventional approach (based on trade-weighted foreign incomes or expenditures) does. The latter approach may bias the estimated income elasticities of U.S. exports up by giving a greater weight to those countries which buy more U.S. exports. In practice, however, the income elasticities of exports estimated in the log-level regressions using other OECD GDP without time trends (equations 5.5 and 5.11 in Table A-5) are comparable to those found in some other studies which used trade-weighted foreign incomes (e.g., Lawrence, 1990) and in Cline's (1989) disaggregated model.

[4] This is the same dependent variable used in most previous studies, such as Krugman and Baldwin (1987) and Helkie and Hooper (1988).

[5] The combination of other OECD GDP with the RX-101 index yields similar results to the same specification with the G-10 index. These results are omitted to save space.

Bibliography

Aguilar Zinser, Adolfo. "México y Estados Unidos hacia el año 2000. Integración silenciosa o alianza concertada." In Lorenzo Meyer, ed., *Anuario de Relaciones México-Estados Unidos.* Mexico City: El Colegio de México, 1989–90.

Alterman, William. "Price Trends in U.S. Trade: New Data, New Insights." In Peter Hooper and J. David Richardson, eds., *International Economic Transactions: Issues in Measurement and Empirical Research.* Chicago: University of Chicago/NBER, 1991, forthcoming.

Amsden, Alice. "Taiwan's Economic History: A Case of Etatisme and a Challenge to Dependency Theory." *Modern China,* Vol. 5, 1979, pp. 341–80.

Amsden, Alice. *Asia's Next Giant: South Korea and Late Industrialization.* Oxford: Oxford University Press, 1989.

Aschauer, David Alan. *Public Investment and Private Sector Growth.* Washington, DC: Economic Policy Institute, 1990.

Balassa, Bela and Marcus Noland. *Japan in the World Economy.* Washington, DC: Institute for International Economics, 1988.

Baldwin, Richard E. "Hysteresis in Import Prices: The Beachhead Effect." *American Economic Review,* Vol. 78, No. 4, September 1988, pp. 773–85.

Baumol, William J., Sue Blackman, and Edward N. Wolff. *Productivity and American Leadership: The Long View.* Cambridge, MA: MIT Press, 1989.

Bazen, Stephen and Tony Thirlwall. *Deindustrialization.* Studies in the UK Economy. Oxford: Heinemann Educational, 1989.

Bernheim, B. Douglas. "Budget Deficits and the Balance of Trade." *Tax Policy and the Economy,* National Bureau of Economic Research, Vol. 2, 1988, pp. 1–31.

Bernheim, B. Douglas. "A Neoclassical Perspective on Budget Deficits." *Journal of Economic Perspectives,* Vol. 3, No. 2, Spring 1989, pp. 55–72.

Blair, Margaret M. and Robert E. Litan. "Corporate Leverage and Leveraged Buyouts in the Eighties." In J. B. Shoven and J. Waldfogel, eds., *Debt, Taxes, and Corporate Restructuring.* Washington, DC: The Brookings Institution, 1990.

Blecker, Robert A. *Are Americans on a Consumption Binge? The Evidence Reconsidered.* Washington, DC: Economic Policy Institute, 1990a.

Blecker, Robert A. "The 'Consumption Binge' Is a Myth." *Challenge,* Vol. 33, No. 3, May/June 1990b, pp. 22–30.

Blecker, Robert A. "Low Saving Rates and the 'Twin Deficits': Confusing the Symptoms and Causes of Economic Decline." In Paul Davidson and Jan A. Kregel, eds., *Economic Problems of the 1990s.* Brookfield, VT: Edward Elgar, 1991a.

Blecker, Robert A. "Profitability and Spending-Saving Behavior in the U.S. Economy: A Test of the Exhilirationist Hypothesis." American University, unpublished paper, January 1991b.

Block, Fred C. "Bad Data Drive Out Good: The Decline of Personal Savings Reexamined." *Journal of Post Keynesian Economics,* Vol. 13, No. 1, Fall 1990, pp. 3–19.

Blomstrom, Magnus and Edward N. Wolff. "Multinational Corporations and Productivity Convergence in Mexico." National Bureau of Economic Research. Working Paper No. 3141, October 1989.

Branson, William H. "Causes of Appreciation and Volatility of the Dollar." In *The U.S. Dollar—Recent Developments, Outlook, and Policy Options.* Kansas City: Federal Reserve Bank of Kansas City, 1985.

Bryant, Ralph C. et al., eds. *Empirical Macroeconomics for Interdependent Economies.* Washington, DC: The Brookings Institution, 1988.

Bryant, Ralph C. and Gerald Holtham. "The External Deficit: Why? Where Next? What Remedy?" *The Brookings Review,* Spring 1987, pp. 28–36.

Cantor, Richard. "Interest Rates, Household Cash Flow, and Consumer Expenditures." Federal Reserve Bank of New York, *Quarterly Review,* Summer 1989, pp. 59–67.

Cline, William R. *United States External Adjustment and the World Economy.* Washington, DC: Institute for International Economics, 1989.

Cooper, Richard. "Symposium on the Causes of the U.S. Trade Deficit." United States General Accounting Office, Report to Congressional Requesters, 1987.

Cypher, James M. *State and Capital in Mexico: Development Policy Since 1940.* Boulder, CO: Westview Press, 1990.

Davidson, Paul. "A Post Keynesian Positive Contribution to 'Theory.'" *Journal of Post Keynesian Economics,* Vol. 13, No. 2, Winter 1990–91, pp. 298–303.

Denison, Edward F. *Estimates of Productivity Change by Industry.* Washington, DC: The Brookings Institution, 1989.

Dernburg, Thomas F. "The Global Debtor-Creditor Relationship: Conflict or Symbiosis?" American University, unpublished paper, November 1989.

Dertouzos, Michael L. et al., eds. *Made in America: Regaining the Productive Edge.* Cambridge, MA: MIT Press, 1989.

Dewald, William G. and Michael Ulan. "The Twin Deficit Illusion." *Cato Journal,* Winter 1990.

Dollar, David and Edward N. Wolff. "Convergence of Industry Labor Productivity Among Advanced Economies, 1963–1982." *Review of Economics and Statistics,* Vol. 70, No. 4, November 1988, pp. 549–58.

Dornbusch, Rudiger. "Expectations and Exchange Rate Dynamics." *Journal of Political Economy,* Vol. 84, December 1976, pp. 1161–76.

Dornbusch, Rudiger. *Dollars, Debts, and Deficits.* Cambridge, MA: MIT Press, 1985.

Dornbusch, Rudiger. "The Adjustment Mechanism: Theory and Problems." In Norman S. Fieleke, ed., *International Payments Imbalances in the 1980s.* Boston, MA: Federal Reserve Bank of Boston, 1988a.

Dornbusch, Rudiger. "Mexico: Stabilization, Debt and Growth." *Economic Policy: A European Forum,* No. 7, October 1988b, pp. 233–83.

Dornbusch, Rudiger. "Commentary." In Albert E. Burger, ed., *U.S. Trade Deficit: Causes, Consequences, and Cures.* Proceedings of the Twelfth Annual Economic Policy Conference of the Federal Reserve Bank of St. Louis (1987). Boston, MA: Kluwer Academic Publishers, 1989a.

Dornbusch, Rudiger. "The Dollar, U.S. Adjustment and the System." Unpublished, MIT, Paper presented at American Economic Association Meetings, Atlanta, GA, December 1989b.

Dornbusch, Rudiger. "Is There a Case For Aggressive Bilateralism and How Best to Practice It?" In Robert Z. Lawrence and Charles L. Schultze, eds., *An American Trade Strategy: Three Options for the 1990s.* Washington, DC: The Brookings Institution, 1990.

Dornbusch, Rudiger, Stanley Fischer, and Paul A. Samuelson. "Comparative Advantage, Trade, and Payments in a Ricardian Model With a Continuum of Goods." *American Economic Review,* Vol. 67, December 1977, pp. 823–39.

Dornbusch, Rudiger, Paul Krugman, and Yung Chul Park. *Meeting World Challenges: U.S. Manufacturing in the 1990s.* Rochester, NY: Eastman Kodak Company, 1989.

Dosi, Giovanni, Keith Pavitt, and Luc Soete. *The Economics of Technical Change and International Trade.* New York: New York University Press, 1990.

Eatwell, John. *Whatever Happened to Britain? The Economics of Decline.* Toronto: Oxford University Press, 1982.

Eichengreen, Barry. "International Competition in the Products of U.S. Basic Industries." In Martin Feldstein, ed., *The United States in the World Economy.* Chicago: University of Chicago Press, 1988.

Eisner, Robert. *Factors in Business Investment.* Cambridge, MA: NBER and Ballinger Books, 1978.

Eisner, Robert. "Budget Deficits: Rhetoric and Reality." *Journal of Economic Perspectives,* Vol. 3, No. 2, Fall 1989, pp. 73–93.

Eisner, Robert. "The Real Rate of U.S. National Saving." *Review of Income and Wealth,* Series 37, March 1991.

Eisner, Robert, and Paul J. Pieper. "The World's Greatest Debtor Nation?" *North American Review of Economics & Finance,* vol. 1, no. 1, 1990, pp. 9–32.

Eisner, Robert, and Paul J. Pieper. "National Saving and the Twin Deficits: Myth and Reality." In James H. Gapinski, ed., *The Economics of Saving.* Boston: Kluwer Academic Publishers, 1992 (forthcoming).

Feinberg, Richard E., John Echeverri-Gent, and Friedemann Müller. *Economic Reform in Three Giants.* New Brunswick, NJ: Transaction Books in cooperation with the Overseas Development Council, 1990.

Feldstein, Martin S. "The Budget Deficit and the Dollar." In *NBER Macroeconomics Annual 1986.* Cambridge, MA: MIT Press, 1986.

Frankel, Jeffrey A. "The Dazzling Dollar." *Brooking Papers on Economic Activity,* No. 1, 1985, pp. 199–217.

Frankel, Jeffrey A. "The Making of Exchange Rate Policy in the 1980s." National Bureau of Economic Research. Working Paper No. 3539, December 1990.

Frankel, Jeffrey A. and Kenneth Froot. "Exchange Rate Forecasting Techniques, Survey Data, and Implications for the Foreign Exchange Market." International Monetary Fund. Working Paper No. 90/43, May 1990.

Freeman, Christopher. *The Economics of Industrial Innovation.* Cambridge, MA: MIT Press, 1982.

Frenkel, Jacob A. "Commentary on 'Causes of Appreciation and Volatility of the Dollar.'" In *The U.S. Dollar—Recent Developments, Outlook, and Policy Options.* Kansas City: Federal Reserve Bank of Kansas City, 1985.

Friedman, Benjamin M. "Lessons on Monetary Policy from the 1980s." *Journal of Economic Perspectives,* Vol. 2, No. 3, Summer 1988, pp. 51–72.

Frischtak, Claudio R. "Structural Change and Trade in Brazil and the Newly Industrializing Latin American Economies." In Randal B. Purcell, ed., *The Newly Industrializing Countries in the World Economy: Challenges for U.S. Policy.* Boulder and London: Lynne Rienner Publishers, 1989.

Fröbel, Folker, Jürgen Heinrichs, and Otto Kreye. *The New International Division of Labour.* Cambridge, MA: Cambridge University Press, 1980.

Galbraith, James K. and Paulo Du Pin Calmon. "Relative Wages and International Competitiveness in U.S. Industry." In Peter Albin and Eileen Appelbaum, eds., *Information Technology: Economic and Policy Implications.* Armonk, NY: M.E. Sharpe Publishers, Inc., forthcoming.

Goldstein, Henry N. "Should We Fret About Our Low Net National Saving Rate?" U.S. Department of State, Bureau of Economic and Business Affairs. PAS Working Paper WP/90/19, July 1990.

Graham, Edward M. and Paul R. Krugman. *Foreign Direct Investment in the United States.* Washington, DC: Institute for International Economics, 1989.

Greider, William. *Secrets of the Temple.* New York: Simon and Schuster, 1987.

Hatsopoulos, George N., Paul R. Krugman, and Lawrence H. Summers. "U.S. Competitiveness: Beyond the Trade Deficit." *Science,* Vol. 241, July 15, 1988, pp. 299–307.

Hatsopoulos, George N., Paul R. Krugman, and James M. Poterba. *Overconsumption: The Challenge to U.S. Economic Policy.* New York and Washington: American Business Conference and Thermo Electron Corporation, 1989.

Helkie, William L. and Peter Hooper. "An Empirical Analysis of the External Deficit." In Ralph C. Bryant et al., eds., *External Deficits and the Dollar: The Pit and the Pendulum.* Washington, DC: The Brookings Institution, 1988.

Hooper, Peter. "U.S. Net Foreign Saving Has Also Plunged." *Challenge,* July-August 1989, pp. 33–38.

Hooper, Peter and Kathryn A. Larin. "International Comparisons of Labor Costs in Manufacturing." *Review of Income and Wealth,* Series 35, December 1989.

Hooper, Peter and Catherine L. Mann. "Exchange Rate Pass-through in the 1980s: The Case of U.S. Imports of Manufactures." *Brookings Papers on Economic Activity,* No. 1, 1989a, pp. 297–337.

Hooper, Peter and Catherine L. Mann. "The U.S. External Deficit: Its Causes and Persistence." In Albert E. Burger, ed., *U.S. Trade Deficit: Causes, Consequences, and Cures.* Proceedings of the Twelfth Annual Economic Policy Conference of the Federal Reserve Bank of St. Louis (1987). Boston, MA: Kluwer Academic Publishers, 1989b.

Houthakker, Hendrik S. and Stephen P. Magee, "Income and Price Elasticities in World Trade." *Review of Economics and Statistics,* Vol. 51, May 1969, pp. 111–25.

Hufbauer, Gary C. "Floating Exchange Rates, Trade Deficits, and Budget Deficits." Testimony before U.S. Senate, Committee on Finance, Subcommittee on Trade, April 23, 1985.

Inter-American Development Bank. *Economic and Social Progress in Latin America: 1989 Report.* Washington, DC, 1989.

International Monetary Fund (IMF). *International Financial Statistics.* Washington, DC: IMF, various issues.

Johnson, Chalmers. *MITI and the Japanese Miracle: The Growth of Industrial Policy, 1925–1975.* Stanford, CA: Stanford University Press, 1982.

Karier, Thomas. *Trade Deficits and Labor Unions: Myths and Realities.* Washington, DC: Economic Policy Institute, 1990.

Kreinin, Mordechai E. "How Closed is the Japanese Market? Additional Evidence." *The World Economy,* Vol. 11, No. 4, December 1988.

Krueger, Anne O. "Free Trade is the Best Policy." In Robert Z. Lawrence and Charles L. Schultze, eds., *An American Trade Strategy: Three Options for the 1990s.* Washington, DC: The Brookings Institution, 1990.

Krugman, Paul R. "A Model of Innovation, Technology Transfer, and the World Distribution of Income." *Journal of Political Economy,* Vol. 87, No. 2, April 1979, pp. 253–66.

Krugman, Paul R. *Exchange-Rate Instability.* Cambridge, MA: MIT Press, 1989.

Krugman, Paul R. and Richard E. Baldwin. "The Persistence of the U.S. Trade Deficit." *Brookings Papers on Economic Activity,* No. 1, 1987, pp. 1–43.

Krugman, Paul R. and Maurice Obstfeld. *International Economics: Theory and Policy.* Boston, MA: Scott, Foresman, and Company, 1988.

Kuttner, Robert. *Managed Trade and Economic Sovereignty.* Washington, DC: Economic Policy Institute, 1989.

Lawrence, Robert Z. "Imports in Japan: Closed Markets or Minds?" *Brookings Papers on Economic Activity,* No. 2, 1987, pp. 517–54.

Lawrence, Robert Z. "The International Dimension." In Robert E. Litan et al., eds., *American Living Standards: Threats and Challenges.* Washington, DC: The Brookings Institution, 1989.

Lawrence, Robert Z. "U.S. Current Account Adjustment: An Appraisal." *Brookings Papers on Economic Activity,* No. 2, 1990, pp. 343–89.

Lawrence, Robert Z. and Robert E. Litan. "The Protectionist Prescription: Errors in Diagnosis and Cure." *Brookings Papers on Economic Activity,* No. 1, 1987, pp. 289–310.

Lessard, Donald R. and John Williamson. *Capital Flight and Third World Debt.* Washington, DC: Institute for International Economics, 1987.

Levich, Richard M. "Financial Innovations in International Financial Markets." In M. Feldstein, ed., *The United States in the World Economy.* Chicago, IL: University of Chicago Press/NBER, 1988.

Lipsey, Robert E. and Irving B. Kravis. *Saving and Economic Growth: Is the United States Really Falling Behind?* New York: The Conference Board, 1987.

Lovett, William A. "Solving the U.S. Trade Deficit and Competitiveness Problem." *Journal of Economic Issues,* Vol. 22, No. 2, June 1988, pp. 459–67.

Luria, Daniel. *Beyond Free Trade and Protectionism: The Public Interest in a U.S. Auto Policy.* Washington, DC: Economic Policy Institute, 1989.

Lustig, Nora. "Economic Crisis, Adjustment and Living Standards in Mexico, 1982–85." *World Development,* Vol. 18, No. 10, October 1990a, pp. 1325–42.

Lustig, Nora. Prepared Testimony on the Agreement Signed by Mexico and Its Commercial Banks, U.S. Congress, House Committee on Banking, Finance, and Urban Affairs, Subcommittee on International Development, Finance, Trade, and Monetary Policy, February 7, 1990b.

Maddison, Angus and Bart van Ark. "International Comparisons of Purchasing Power, Real Output, and Labour Productivity: A Case Study of Brazilian, Mexican, and U.S. Manufacturing." *Review of Income and Wealth,* Series 35, March 1989, pp. 1–30.

Mann, Catherine L. "Prices, Profit Margins and Exchange Rates." *Federal Reserve Bulletin,* Vol. 72, June 1986, pp. 366–79.

Marris, Stephen. *Deficits and the Dollar: The World Economy at Risk.* Washington, DC: Institute for International Economics, December 1985.

Marston, Richard C. "Price Behavior in Japanese and U.S. Manufacturing." National Bureau of Economic Research. Working Paper No. 3364, May 1990.

McCulloch, Rachel. "Trade Deficits, Industrial Competitiveness, and the Japanese." *California Management Review,* Vol. 27, No. 2, 1985, pp. 140–56; reprinted in Robert E. Baldwin and J. David Richardson, eds., *International Trade and Finance: Readings,* Third Edition. Boston, MA: Little and Brown, 1986.

McCulloch, Rachel and J. David Richardson. "U.S. Trade and the Dollar: Evaluating Current Policy Options." In Robert E. Baldwin and J. David Richardson, eds., *Current U.S. Trade Policy: Analysis, Agenda, and Administration.* Cambridge, MA: NBER, 1986.

McIntyre, Robert S. "Inequality and the Federal Budget Deficit." In Bruce L. Fisher and Robert S. McIntyre, eds., *Growth and Equity: Tax Policy Challenges for the 1990s.* Washington, DC: Citizens for Tax Justice, 1990.

McKibbin, Warwick J. and Jeffrey D. Sachs. "The McKibbin-Sachs Global Model: Theory and Specification." National Bureau of Economic Research. Working Paper No. 3100, 1989.

Mead, Walter Russell. *The Low-Wage Challenge to Global Growth.* Washington, DC: Economic Policy Institute, 1990.

Meade, Ellen E. "Computers and the Trade Deficit: The Case of the Falling Prices." Federal Reserve System, Board of Governors. International Finance Discussion Paper No. 378, April 1990.

Meese, Richard. "Currency Fluctuations in the Post-Bretton Woods Era." *Journal of Economic Perspectives,* Vol. 4, No. 1, Winter 1990, pp. 117–34.

Michl, Thomas R. "Debt, Deficits, and the Distribution of Income. *Journal of Post Keynesian Economics,* Vol. 13, No. 3, Spring 1991, pp. 351–65.

Mishel, Lawrence. *Manufacturing Numbers: How Inaccurate Statistics Conceal U.S. Industrial Decline.* Washington, DC: Economic Policy Institute, 1988.

Mishel, Lawrence and David M. Frankel. *The State of Working America, 1990–91 Edition.* New York: M.E. Sharpe Publishers, Inc., 1991.

Mishel, Lawrence and Ruy Teixeira. *The Myth of the Coming Labor Shortage: Jobs, Skills, and Incomes of America's Workforce 2000.* Washington, DC: Economic Policy Institute, 1991.

Moreno, Ramon. "Exchange Rates and Trade Adjustment in Taiwan and Korea." *Economic Review,* Federal Reserve Bank of San Francisco, Spring 1989, pp. 30–44.

Morgan Guarantee Trust Co., *World Financial Markets,* various issues.

Mowery, David C. and Nathan Rosenberg. "New Developments in U.S. Technology Policy: Implications for Competitiveness and International Trade Policy." *California Management Review,* Vol. 32, No. 1, Fall 1989.

Organization for Economic Cooperation and Development (OECD), *National Accounts, Quarterly National Accounts, Main Economic Indicators, Statistics of Foreign Trade: Monthly Bulletin,* and *Monthly Statistics of Foreign Trade,* Paris: OECD, various issues.

Park, Yung Chul and Won Am Park. "Changing Japanese Trade Patterns and the East Asian NICs" Korean Development Institute. Working Paper, 1990.

Pastor, Manuel, Jr. *Capital Flight and the Latin American Debt Crisis.* Washington, DC: Economic Policy Institute, 1989.

Pauls, B. Dianne. "Measuring the Foreign-Exchange Value of the Dollar." *Federal Reserve Bulletin,* Vol. 73, No. 6, June 1987, pp. 411–22.

Pechman, Joseph A. "The Future of the Income Tax." *American Economic Review,* Vol. 80, No. 1, March 1990, pp. 1–20.

Porter, Michael E. "The Competitive Advantage of Nations." *Harvard Business Review,* Vol. 90, No. 2, March-April 1990, pp. 73–93.

Prestowitz, Clyde V., Jr. *Trading Places: How We Allowed Japan to Take the Lead.* New York: Basic Books, Inc., 1988.

Price, Lee. "Trade Problems and Policy From a U.S. Labor Perspective." In Robert E. Baldwin and J. David Richardson, eds., *Current U.S. Trade Policy: Analysis, Agenda, and Administration.* Cambridge, MA: NBER, 1986.

Quinn, Kevin. "False Promises: Why the Bush Capital Gains Cuts Would Not Result In More Saving, Investment, Economic Growth, or Jobs." Washington, DC: Economic Policy Institute, 1990.

Reich, Robert B. "Bailout: A Comparative Study in Law and Industrial Structure." In A. Michael Spence and Heather A. Hazard, eds., *International Competitiveness.* Cambridge, MA: Ballinger Books, 1988.

Reich, Robert B. "Who Is Us?" *Harvard Business Review,* Vol. 90, No. 1, January-February 1990, pp. 53–64.

Rosenberg, Nathan. *Perspectives on Technology.* Cambridge, MA: Cambridge University Press, 1976.

Rosenberg, Nathan. *Inside The Black Box: Technology and Economics.* Cambridge, MA: Cambridge University Press, 1982.

Sachs, Jeffrey D. "Global Adjustments to a Shrinking U.S. Trade Deficit." *Brookings Papers on Economic Activity,* No. 2, 1988, pp. 639–74.

Sachs, Jeffrey D., ed. *Developing Country Debt and the World Economy.* Chicago, IL: The University of Chicago Press, 1989.

Salvatore, Dominick. *The Japanese Trade Challenge and the U.S. Response: Addressing the Structural Causes of the Bilateral Trade Imbalance.* Washington, DC: Economic Policy Institute, 1990.

Smith, Stephen C. *Industrial Policy and Export Success: Third World Development Strategies Reconsidered.* Washington, DC: Economic Policy Institute, 1991, forthcoming.

Soete, Luc. "International Diffusion of Technology, Industrial Development and Technological Leapfrogging." *World Development,* Vol. 13, No. 3, 1985, pp. 409–22.

Steindl, Josef. "Capital Gains, Pension Funds, and the Low Saving Ratio in the United States." *Banca Nazionale del Lavoro Quarterly Review,* June 1990, pp. 165–77.

Summers, Lawrence H. "Tax Policy and International Competitiveness." In Jacob A. Frenkel, ed., *International Aspects of Fiscal Policies.* Chicago, IL: University of Chicago Press, 1988.

Szirmai, Adam and Dirk Pilat. "Comparisons of Purchasing Power, Real Output and Labour Productivity in Manufacturing in Japan, South Korea, and the U.S.A., 1975–85." *Review of Income and Wealth,* Series 36, No. 1, March 1990, pp. 1–31.

Taylor, Lance. *Structuralist Macroeconomics.* New York: Basic Books, 1983.

Taylor, Lance. "A Stagnationist Model of Economic Growth." *Cambridge Journal of Economics,* Vol. 9, No. 4, December 1985, pp. 383–403.

Taylor, Lance. *Varieties of Stabilization Experience: Towards Sensible Macroeconomics in the Third World.* Oxford: Clarendon Press, 1988.

Thirlwall, A.P. "The Balance of Payments Constraint as an Explanation of International Growth Rate Differences." *Banca Nazionale del Lavoro Quarterly Review,* No. 128, March 1979, pp. 45–53.

Todaro, Michael. *Economic Development in the Third World,* Fourth Edition. New York: Longman, 1989.

United Nations, Economic Commission on Latin America and the Caribbean

(UN/ECLAC). *Latin America and the Caribbean. Options to Reduce the Debt Burden.* Santiago, Chile, February 1990.

U.S. Congress, Congressional Budget Office. "Potential Effects of NIPA Rebasing and GPO Revisions in 1990 and 1991 on Perceptions of Real Growth in the 1980s." CBO Staff Memorandum, April 1990.

U.S. Congress, Joint Economic Committee. "Restoring International Balance: Japan's Trade and Investment Patterns." Staff Study, July 1988.

U.S. Council of Economic Advisors. *Economic Report of the President,* Washington, DC: U.S. Government Printing Office, various years.

U.S. Department of Commerce, Bureau of Economic Analysis. *Business Statistics 1961–88.* Washington, DC: U.S. Government Printing Office, December 1989.

U.S. Department of Commerce, Bureau of Economic Analysis. *The National Income and Product Accounts of the United States, 1929–82: Statistical Tables,* and *Survey of Current Business,* various issues.

U.S. Department of Commerce, Bureau of the Census, Foreign Trade Division, U.S. Merchandise Trade. Report FT990, Washington, DC: Government Printing Office, various issues.

U.S. Department of Commerce, International Trade Administration, Office of Trade and Investment Analysis. U.S. High Tech Trade, unpublished data, 1989.

U.S. Department of Labor, Bureau of Labor Statistics. *Handbook of Labor Statistics.* Washington, DC: U.S. Government Printing Office, August 1989.

U.S. Department of Labor, Bureau of Labor Statistics. "International Comparisons of Hourly Compensation Costs for Production Workers in Manufacturing, 1975–89." Report 794, October 1990a.

U.S. Department of Labor, Bureau of Labor Statistics. "International Comparisons of Manufacturing Productivity and Labor Cost Trends, 1989," July 1990b.

U.S. Federal Reserve Bank of Dallas, Research Department. Trade-Weighted Value of the Dollar, various releases.

U.S. Federal Reserve System, Board of Governors. Foreign Exchange Rates, various releases.

U.S. General Accounting Office. *U.S. Trade Deficit: Impact of Currency Appreciations in Taiwan, South Korea, and Hong Kong.* Report No. GAO/NSIAD-89-130, April 1989.

U.S. International Trade Commission. *The Likely Impact on the United States of a Free Trade Agreement with Mexico.* Report to the Committee on Ways and Means of the U.S. House of Representatives and the Committee on Finance of the U.S. Senate. Publication No. 2353, February 1991.

U.S. National Science Foundation. *National Patterns of R&D Resources, 1990.* Report 90-316, Washington, DC: National Science Foundation, 1990.

Vernon, Raymond. "International Investment and International Trade in the Product Cycle." *Quarterly Journal of Economics,* Vol. 80, May 1966, pp. 190–207.

Wachtel, Howard M. *The Money Mandarins: The Making Of A Supranational Economic Order.* New York: Pantheon Books, 1986.

Williamson, John. "Exchange Rate Management: The Role of Target Zones." *American Economic Review Readings,* Vol. 77, No. 2, May 1987, pp. 200–04.

Wolfson, Martin. *Financial Crises.* New York: M.E. Sharpe Publishers, Inc., 1986.

World Bank, *World Development Report,* 1987 and 1990.

Wright, Gavin. "The Origins of American Industrial Success, 1879–1940." *American Economic Review,* Vol. 80, No. 4, September 1990, pp. 651–68.

Young, Allan, H. "BEA's Measurement of Computer Output." *Survey of Current Business,* July 1989, pp. 108–15.

Index

Deutschmark (German currency), 91, 92, 118
Differencing, 66
Dollar, David, 87
Dollar (Taiwanese), 105, 107–108
Dollar (U.S.)
  depreciation, 131–132
  effects of overvalued, 46–49
  falling trend of, 58–62
  and monetary policy, 42–46
  relative value of, 91
  real value, 60, 62
Domestic content legislation, 118
Dornsbusch, Rudiger, 26, 54*n.2*, 94–95, 114*n.3*, 117
Dosi, Giovanni, 27, 76

E

East Asian NICs, 104–110
Eastern Europe, 126–127
East Germany, 117–118
EC. *See* European Community (EC)
Economic Recovery Tax Act (ERTA), 43
Economic Report of the President, 74
The Economics of Technical Change (Dosi et al.), 29
Eichengreen, Barry, 17–18
Employment, 20, 31*n.4*, 51
Energy, 77–78, 80*n.4*, 127–129
ERTA. *See* Economic Recovery Tax Act (ERTA)
Europe, 40
European Community (EC), 117–118
Exchange rate, 22–27, 62, 71, 119
  macro policies and, 91–97, 129–132

Exchange rate *(continued)*
  real German and Japanese, 92
  South Korean policy, 106
  Taiwanese policy, 109
  U.S. policy, 131–132
Expansionary fiscal policy, 33–38, 54*n.4*
Export demand equations, 65–68
Export-led growth, 104, 121

F

Federal Reserve Bank, 42–43, 46, 60
Federal Reserve Board, 49, 60
Four Tigers, 99
France, 82
Frankel, Jeffrey A., 44
Free trade area (FTA), 124–126

G

G-10 index, 60–61
GATT. *See* General Agreement on Trade and Tariffs (GATT)
GDP. *See* gross domestic product (GDP)
General Accounting Office, 105
General Agreement on Trade and Tariffs (GATT), 121
General System of Preferences (GSP), 136*n.5*
Germany. *See* East Germany; West Germany
Gross domestic product (GDP), 38–42

About the Author

Robert A. Blecker is Assistant Professor of Economics at American University, Washington, DC, and a Fellow at the Economic Policy Institute (EPI). His research on international competition, income distribution, and industrial decline has been published in the *Cambridge Journal of Economics*, the *Journal of Post Keynesian Economics*, and the *International Review of Applied Economics*. He has also written a series of articles on consumption and saving behavior in the U.S. economy, including an EPI report entitled *Are Americans on a Consumption Binge? The Evidence Reconsidered.*

The Economic Policy Institute was founded in 1986 to widen the debate about policies to acheive healthy economic growth, prosperity, and opportunity in the difficult new era America has entered.

Today, America's economy is threatened by stagnant growth and increasing inequality. Expanding global competition, changes in the nature of work, and rapid technological advances are altering economic reality. Yet many of our policies, attitudes, and institutions are based on assumptions that no longer reflect real world conditions.

Central to the Economic Policy Institute's search for solutions is the exploration of the economics of teamwork—economic policies that encourage every segment of the American economy (business, labor, government, universities, voluntary organizations, etc.) to work cooperatively to raise productivity and living standards for all Americans. Such an undertaking involves a challenge to conventional views of market behavior and a revival of a cooperative relationship between the public and private sectors.

With the support of leaders from labor, business, and the foundation world, the Institute has sponsored research and public discussion of a wide variety of topics: trade and fiscal policies; trends in wages, incomes, and prices; the causes of the productivity slowdown; labor market problems; U.S. and Third World debt; rural and urban policies; inflation; state-level economic development strategies; comparative international economic performance; and studies of the overall health of the U.S. manufacturing sector and of specific key industries.

The Institute works with a growing network of innovative economists and other social science researchers in universities and research centers all over the country who are willing to go beyond the conventional wisdom in considering strategies for public policy.

The research committee of the Institute includes:

Jeff Faux—EPI President
Lester Thurow—Dean of MIT's Sloan School of Management
Ray Marshall—former U.S. Secretary of Labor, currently a Professor at the LBJ School of Public Affairs, University of Texas
Barry Bluestone—University of Massachusetts-Boston
Robert Reich—JFK School of Government, Harvard University
Robert Kuttner—Author; columnist, *New Republic,* and *Business Week;* co-editor, *New Republic*

EPI Reports, Working Papers, Briefing Papers, and Seminars are distributed by *Public Interest Publications.* For a publications list or to order, call 1-800-537-9359.

Other **EPI Books** are available from ME Sharpe at 1-800-541-6563.

For additional information contact the Institute / 1730 Rhode Island Ave., NW, Suite 200 / Washington, DC 20036 / 202-775-8810.